MCQs
FOR THE
MRCS EXAMS

MCQs FOR THE MRCS EXAMS

Mr KM Reddy, BSc, MBBS, LLB, FRCS (Eng)
Clinical Research Fellow in Surgery, University Department of Surgery, St George's Hospital Medical School, London

Mr FF Palazzo, MD, FRCSI, FRCS (Eng)
Specialist Registrar in General Surgery, Anglia and Oxford (Addenbrooke's) Deanery

A. I. T. B. S.

2000

A.I.T.B.S. Publishers & Distributors (Regd.)
J-5/6, KRISHAN NAGAR, DELHI-110 051 (INDIA)
Phone : 2460494, 2054798, 2249313
Fax : 011-2243416, 2218401

Cavendish Publishing Limited, U.K., ISBN-1-85941-402-8
AITBS Publishers, India ISBN -81-7473-121-0

2000

First Indian Edition 2000

Original Edition Published by :
Cavendish Publishing Limited, U.K.

This edition has been published in India by arrangement with Cavendish Publishing Limited, U.K. for sale in India

A CIP catalogue record for this book is available from the British Library.

Published by Virender Kumar Arya for
A.I.T.B.S. Publishers & Distributors (Regd.)
J-5/6, Krishan Nagar, Delhi-110 051 and
Printed by Sanjeev Offset Printers, Delhi

Foreword

Preparing for an examination is usually a time of intense commitment, self-doubt and fatigue. We need all the help we can get at such moments in our careers and this is even more the case when the circumstance of an examination are novel. This book is a companion in two senses. First, it follows closely the syllabus for the MRCS (AFRCS in Edinburgh) diploma. This syllabus can be found in the regulations published by the Royal Colleges, an up to date version of which should be consulted by all candidates as the examination continues to evolve. The syllabus is covered in the well received STEP course available from the College of Surgeons of England. During learning it is always a good idea to test one's grasp of the topic and this book acts also as a study comparison with a wide range of MCQ's against which to test your knowledge.

After 20 months of mandatory training and the MCQ under your belt you can proceed to the next step of the examination – the vivas. Here too you will find some helpful hints as to how to approach the later stages of the examination – though the long case (in the clinical examination later) is now consigned to history.

With best wishes for your endeavours.

David Ralphs
Member of the Court of Examiners
Royal College of Surgeons, England
Regional Advisor in Surgery for Anglia

Preface

Basic Surgical Training (BST) has been transformed from an apprenticeship to a structured course. The Applied Basic Science paper and Clinical Surgery in General Examination of the FRCS have been modified to reflect this change. The integration of the basic sciences and clinical topics has lead to the Core modules and System modules of the new MRCS examination.

This book contains 200 MCQs with 1,000 specific questions covering the whole syllabus of the MRCS examination. The questions are grouped in the same fashion as in the syllabus to facilitate self-assessment prior to the MCQ and viva examination.

Candidates who are successful in the multiple choice examinations will be examined in a viva voce examination covering all aspects of surgery and a clinical examination. This part of the exam is designed to assess the ability of the candidate to apply their knowledge. It is essential to understand the questions asked and hence what is required. A chapter on viva techniques and approaches to standard types of questions is included.

We would like to thank those who have given us support and guidance during our training. In particular, we gratefully acknowledge the help of Mr MJ Knight, Professor J Hermon-Taylor, Mr MWE Morgan and Mr RG Springall.

KM Reddy
FF Palazzo
December 1997

CONTENTS

CORE MODULE 3

CORE MODULE 4

CORE MODULE 5

SYSTEM MODULE E

TIPS FOR THE VIVA VOCE EXAMINATION

CORE MODULE 1

PERI-OPERATIVE MANAGEMENT 1

UNIT 1 PERI-OPERATIVE MANAGEMENT

1 The following negatively affect operative risk:

(a) urgency of operation

(b) age

(c) presence of a pacemaker

(d) Goldman Class III

(e) mitral valve area < 3 cm^2

2 A 50 year old patient undergoing elective anterior resection for malignancy requires:

(a) an APTT

(b) a peak expiratory flow rate

(c) electrocardiogram

(d) urea and electrolytes

(e) a chest X-ray

1 (a) T
(b) T
(c) F
(d) T
(e) F

The urgency of an operation may limit the time available for pre-operative preparation. Physiological reserve decreases with age. Impairment of one or more organ systems and the degree of impairment influences operative mortality as assessed by the ASA classification. Risk for cardiac complications in non cardiac surgery are assessed by the Goldman criteria. Goldman Class III is associated with 11% life threatening complications and 3% deaths. Mitral stenosis is symptomatic only when the valve area is < 2.5 cm^2.

2 (a) F
(b) F
(c) T
(d) T
(e) T

A pre-operative full blood count is requested in all major surgery and in all menstruating women. Urea and electrolytes are required in all patients over the age of 50 years and those with coexistent disease (cardiovascular, renal, endocrine disorders) or on drugs that may alter the serum concentrations (diuretics, steroids). Chest radiography is indicated in patients over 50 years or those with cardiac or respiratory disease. In this case surgery for malignancy is an indication per se.

3 The following are methods controlling coexistent disease pre-operatively:

(a) monoamine oxidase inhibitors in established hypertension

(b) phenoxybenzamine in thyrotoxicosis

(c) Swann-Ganz catheter in congestive cardiac failure

(d) antibiotics in jaundiced patients

(e) 20% mannitol prior to clipping of anterior communicating artery aneurysms

4 Renal function is assessed by:

(a) an intravenous pyelogram

(b) DTPA scan

(c) DMSA scan

(d) Inulin clearance

(e) Mag 3 scan

5 The malnourished patient is assessed by:

(a) anthropometric measurements

(b) biceps girth

(c) albumin levels

(d) dietary history

(e) transferrin levels

3 (a) F
(b) F
(c) F
(d) T
(e) F

Monoamine oxidase inhibitors interact with anaesthetic drugs and are contraindicated in surgery. Phenoxybenzamine is an α blocker used to prepare patients with phaeochromocytoma. Jaundiced patients are susceptible to sepsis. Mannitol is used to reduce intracranial hypertension.

4 (a) F
(b) T
(c) T
(d) T
(e) T

Intravenous pyelograms demonstrate anatomical integrity. DTPA assesses renal perfusion. DMSA serves to assess tubular function. MAG 3 scans offer both perfusion and tubular function information. Clearance is the measurement of the amount of plasma cleared of a substance in unit time. Inulin is used because it is all excreted.

5 (a) T
(b) F
(c) T
(d) T
(e) T

A detailed dietary history and general examination are in practice the most important factors in the nutritional assessment of a patient. Anthropometric measurements including height and skin fold thickness and serum concentrations of proteins may be used to confirm malnourishment.

UNIT 2 INFECTION

1 The following reduce wound infection in bowel surgery:

(a) steri-drape
(b) 5 days of antibiotics rather than 3 doses
(c) 2 sachets of Sodium Picosulphate 24 hours pre-op
(d) ante-grade colonic lavage
(e) chlorhexidine shower pre-operatively

2 Antibiotic prophylaxis is given:

(a) in cholecystectomy
(b) in thyroidectomy
(c) to pregnant women in all general anaesthetic procedures
(d) to HIV positive patients undergoing haemorrhoidectomy
(e) in elbow replacement surgery

1 (a) F
(b) F
(c) F
(d) F
(e) F

No evidence exists to indicate that sterile adhesive drapes, prolonged antibiotic prophylaxis, bowel preparation or colonic lavage reduce the incidence of wound infections in bowel surgery. The microbes responsible for wound infections in gut surgery are endogenous (E coli, Bacteroides fragilis, klebsiella etc), rather than of skin origin.

2 (a) T
(b) F
(c) F
(d) F
(e) T

Prophylactic antibiotics are indicated in dirty (large bowel surgery), contaminated (appendicitis, 'hot' cholecystectomies) and clean-contaminated operations. They are also required in clean surgery (infection rate < 2%) where the consequences are severe or life threatening (cardiac valve surgery, limb prosthesis). Pregnant women are at no greater risk of wound infection than the general population and caution is recommended for all drugs in pregnancy.

3 Sterilisation:

(a) is the elimination of all surgically relevant pathogens

(b) may be achieved with an autoclave at 121°C for 3 minutes

(c) is checked by Bowie Dick test which is a biological indicator

(d) must be present in skin prior to incision

(e) can be achieved with Ethylene oxide at room temperature

4 The following are special precautions adopted on high risk patients:

(a) antibiotic prophylaxis

(b) no touch technique

(c) transit trays and dishes

(d) laminar airflow

(e) last on operating list

5 Clostridium perfringens is:

(a) gram positive

(b) an obligate aerobe

(c) spore forming

(d) positive for the Nagler test

(e) is the commonest cause of amputation in war

3 (a) F
(b) F
(c) F
(d) F
(e) T

Sterilisation is the removal of all organisms including heat resistant spores. Steam jacketed autoclaves achieve sterility at 134°C for 3 minutes. Thermophilus spp is the biological indicator used in the sterilisation process. Sterilization of the skin cannot be achieved without damage to its structure hence the skin is 'prepared' with elimination of up to 99% of organisms. Ethylene oxide is used in few centres eg St Thomas' Hospital, London but carries the disadvantage of the need for prolonged ventilation.

4 (a) F
(b) T
(c) T
(d) F
(e) F

Patients that are identified as presenting a high risk of contamination (eg patients with hepatitis or HIV) merit special precautions. In some centres, especially those with a high prevalence of risk patients special precautions are adopted in all cases. The precautions include waterproof drapes and surgical gowns, goggles, double gloving or kevlar gloves, use of a transit dish for sharps, use of diathermy in preference to scalpel and the use of staples. Patients known to present a particularly high risk should be put first on the list, the rationale is that this is when the surgeon and other staff are most alert and therefore accidents are less likely to happen.

5 (a) T
(b) F
(c) T
(d) T
(e) F

Clostridium difficile is a gram positive spore forming obligate anaerobe of great surgical significance. It is responsible for gas gangrene. The Nagler test is diagnostic. The commonest cause of amputation in wartime are vascular injuries.

UNIT 3 INVESTIGATIVE AND OPERATIVE PROCEDURES

1 Causes of anastomotic leakage are:

(a) failure to prepare bowel
(b) one layer of suture
(c) malnutrition
(d) tension
(e) failure to use a drain

2 The following statements regarding sutures are true:

(a) braided are stronger than monofilament
(b) the half-life of cat gut is 9 days
(c) polypropolene has memory
(d) using linen avoids granulomas
(e) polydioxanone is absorbable

3 Histological diagnosis may be achieved by:

(a) surgical extirpation
(b) fine needle aspiration
(c) urinalysis
(d) immunohistochemistry
(e) pulmonary brushings

1 (a) F
(b) F
(c) T
(d) T
(e) F

The causes of anastomotic leakage are local and systemic. The local causes are poor blood supply and tension at the site of anastomosis. The systemic factors include malnutrition, immunosuppression, vascular disease and drugs such as steroids. Drains may be responsible for anastomotic breakdown rather than preventing them.

2 (a) T
(b) T
(c) T
(d) F
(e) T

One of the key characteristics of braided sutures is their strength. Plain Catgut loses half of its strength in 8 to 14 days. Polydioxanone (PDS) loses strength in 50 to 60 days and is reabsorbed in 180 days.

3 (a) T
(b) F
(c) F
(d) T
(e) F

Histology implies the microscopic analysis of tissues. It is to be distinguished from cytology eg fine needle aspiration, bronchial brushings and urine microscopy which uses the appearance of cells alone rather than their organisation into tissues to aid in diagnosis. Immunohistochemistry can only be performed accurately on histological specimens.

4 Basal cell carcinoma:

(a) is a tumour of keratinocytes

(b) spreads along the lymphatics

(c) is locally invasive

(d) responds to radiotherapy

(e) is more common in the immunosuppressed

5 Collections of pus:

(a) are called abscesses

(b) require treatment with antibiotics

(c) produce sustained pyrexia

(d) are hypoechoic on ultrasound

(e) in the pleural space are called empyemas

4 (a) T
(b) F
(c) T
(d) T
(e) T

Rodent ulcers originate from keratinocytes. It is a slow growing lesion that is locally invasive without lymphatic involvement. Distant metastases are very rare. Transplant patients and AIDS patients are particularly susceptible to BCC.

5 (a) F
(b) F
(c) F
(d) T
(e) T

Only a collection of pus in a newly formed space is an abscess. Collections of pus in anatomically defined spaces (pleura, gall bladder) are called empyemas. A swinging pyrexia is characteristic of collections of pus. The treatment for a collection of pus is to drain it.

UNIT 4 ANAESTHESIA

1 General anaesthesia:

(a) requires rapid sequence induction
(b) has a 17% post-operative complication rate
(c) may be performed by hypnosis
(d) includes relaxation
(e) is the commonest cause of peri-operative mortality

2 Pre-medication:

(a) includes maintenance of intercurrent medication
(b) reduces anxiety
(c) is administered in the anaesthetic room
(d) with glycopyrrolate dries secretions
(e) is essential in moribund patients

3 Bupivacaine:

(a) is an Ester
(b) must not exceed 225 mg
(c) is commonly used in epidural analgesia
(d) is more toxic than Prilocaine
(e) has a high affinity for cardiac muscle cells

1 (a) F
(b) T
(c) F
(d) T
(e) F

Rapid sequence or crash' induction is required in those cases where there is a high risk of vomiting and aspiration of gastric contents, eg in the non starved patient. Nausea and vomiting are complications of general anaesthesia and occur in 17% of patients. General anaesthesia is the reversible, drug induced state of unresponsiveness with analgesia and relaxation. NCEPOD (1992) reported that anaesthesia contributed to death in 1 in 1,351 cases; it was the sole cause of death in 1 in 185,000 cases.

2 (a) T
(b) T
(c) F
(d) T
(e) F

The aims of pre-medication are anxiolysis, analgesia and the drying of secretions. The drugs used depend on the preference of the anaesthetist and include pethidine, diazepam and glycopyrrolates. These drugs are administered on the ward prior to transport to the operating theatre.

3 (a) F
(b) F
(c) T
(d) T
(e) T

Most local anaesthetics are tertiary amino esters or amides of aromatic acids (bupivacaine). Bupivacaine may be given at a dose of 2 mg/kg and a maximum dose of 150 mg is recommended. It may be given as an epidural infusion and it is more toxic than prilocaine. Local anaesthetics stabilise membrane permeability in the heart and therefore prolong conduction time and depress myocardial excitability thus explaining the possible toxic effects if used inappropriately and underlining the need for monitoring during administration.

4 Muscle relaxation during general anaesthesia:

(a) allows better access to body cavities

(b) is achieved by d-tubocurare in under 1 minute

(c) is required for artificial ventilation

(d) can lead to histamine release

(e) is reversed with Neostigmine and muscarinic agents

5 Patients under general anaesthetic::

(a) are at risk of hyperthermia

(b) require intra-cranial pressure monitoring in neurosurgery

(c) require endo-tracheal intubation

(d) have an overall mortality of 0.7%

(e) are at greater risk of pulmonary embolism than those under regional anaesthesia

4 (a) T
(b) F
(c) T
(d) T
(e) T

The aim of paralysis is to allow better access to body cavities such as the abdomen. These patients require ventilatory support. It may be achieved with non depolarising muscle relaxant drugs such as Atracurium or Vecuronium within 3 minutes and the effect lasts up to one hour. Reversal of paralysed patients with neostigmine and atropine speeds up awakening.

5 (a) F
(b) F
(c) F
(d) T
(e) T

Temperature regulation is poor in the anaesthetised patient with a tendency to hypothermia, which is more marked in children. Laryngeal masks are increasingly used, especially in day case surgery thus avoiding endotracheal intubation. The overall mortality associated with general anaesthesia (NCEPOD 1992) is 0.7%. The risk of pulmonary embolism is related to both intrinsic and extrinsic factors, the latter include the type of anaesthesia.

UNIT 5 THEATRE PROBLEMS

1 The Nucleus Concept recommends the following in operating theatre design:

(a) laminar air flow in all operating theatres

(b) 17 m^2 scrub room

(c) easy access to the accident and emergency department, the surgical wards and the intensive care unit

(d) four clearly demarcated areas

(e) a recovery area that offers 1.5 beds per operating theatre

2 Hazards of diathermy include:

(a) capacitance coupling

(b) arrhythmias in patients with heart disease

(c) tetany

(d) explosion of anaesthetic and bowel gases

(e) damage of appendages

1 (a) F
(b) F
(c) T
(d) T
(e) T

The Department of Health and Social Security attempted in 1978 to introduce a 'standard' operating theatre – the Nucleus Concept. This introduced guidelines to the site, structure and function of the operating theatre. Laminar flow with up to 400 air changes per hour are recommended only in some forms of surgery eg the Charnley tent in orthopaedics. The scrub room need only be 10 square meters. The operating theatre should include an outer zone, a clean zone, an aseptic zone and a dirty zone. The recovery area must be able to accommodate patients immediately after surgery and be equipped with the appropriate monitoring and resuscitation equipment.

2 (a) T
(b) F
(c) F
(d) T
(e) T

Capacitance coupling is a build up of charge at the port-instrument interface that may discharge, and with direct coupling it is one of the hazards of the use of diathermy in laparoscopic surgery. Arrythmias may occur in patients with pacemakers. It is documented that sparks produced by diathermy may ignite inflammable bowel gases. Extremities are at risk during the use of monopolar diathermy, for this reason it is best avoided in procedures such as circumcision.

3 Pulmonary embolism:

(a) is the commonest cause of peri-operative death in orthopaedic surgery

(b) is fatal in 1% of patients

(c) may produce characteristic changes in waves Q, T and S

(d) may present with pyrexia

(e) characteristically occurs 72 hours post-operatively

4 Laser:

(a) is an acronym for light absorption of simulated emitted radiation

(b) use requires a Laser Protection Officer

(c) may be gaseous or crystalline

(d) wavelength determines absorption

(e) is used in palliation of rectal tumours

5 The following are features of operating tables:

(a) a radioluscent section

(b) permanent fixation

(c) adjustable lumbar supports

(d) a mid-table break

(e) removable Sorbo rubber padding

3 (a) T
(b) F
(c) T
(d) T
(e) F

The mortality following pulmonary embolism is as high as 10%. It is characterised in the case of large emboli by SI QIII and TIII changes. PEs may present insidiously with a pyrexia in the absence of respiratory distress and should be borne in mind in the differential diagnosis of post-operative pyrexia. There is no characteristic time of presentation of deep vein thromboses or pulmonary emboli.

4 (a) F
(b) T
(c) T
(d) T
(e) T

LASER stands for Light Amplification by the Stimulated Emission of Radiation and is a highly directional beam of coherent electromagnetic radiation. The laser source may be solid (eg NdYAG) or gaseous (eg argon) and the wavelength emitted by these sources determines the degree of absorption. The hazards are both to the patient and the operator and a laser protection advisor and laser safety officer are required to oversee its use. One of the many current uses of laser is in the prevention of obstruction by tumours invading the lumen of viscera eg oesophagus and rectum.

5 (a) T
(b) F
(c) T
(d) T
(e) T

A radioluscent section is required to allow intra-operative radiographs to be taken eg vascular surgery. Though an operating table should be stable it need not be fixed; indeed mobile tables offer the advantage that the operating theatre may be used even when a table is not functioning due to the ease of replacement. The other features of operating tables such as padding, supports and an angulation of parts of the table are required to allow versatility and safety.

CORE MODULE 2

PERI-OPERATIVE MANAGEMENT 2

UNIT 1 SKIN AND WOUNDS

1 The following associations are true:

(a) Lanz incision for appendicectomy is muscle splitting

(b) Lockwood and femoral hernia repair

(c) left thoracotomy and Ivor Lewis procedure

(d) Jenkin's law and abdominal wound dehiscence

(e) familiarity and keloid scarring

2 Methods of wound cover include:

(a) V-Y-plasty

(b) Wolfman graft

(c) pinch graft in breast reconstruction

(d) liophilised skin

(e) amnion dressing

1 (a) T
(b) T
(c) F
(d) T
(e) T

The appropriate choice of incision is determined by the ability to gain access and exposure, the ease of extension, speed and cosmesis. Closure with suture one centimeter apart and one centimeter from the wound edge ensure a low risk of 'cut through' in abdominal wound closure. Enzymes catalyse the breakdown of tissue around the suture. Hypertrophic scarring in contrast to keloid scarring resolves after 6 months and does not extend beyond the wound edge. Risk of keloid scarring is directly proportional to the number of melanocytes in the skin and has a familial tendency.

2 (a) T
(b) F
(c) F
(d) T
(e) T

The hierarchy of plastic surgical cover begins with simple suture where a clean, tension free wound exists. Delayed primary and secondary closure, and then the use of split or full thickness skin grafting. Composite grafts such as myocutaneous or osseocutaneous may be distant or local. Specific types of local grafts are rotation or advancement; distant grafts may be pedicled and radial osseocutaneous. Tension may be reduced by elongation of the wound length by Z-plasty.

3 The following are true about wounds:

(a) wound contracture does not occur in wounds that are healing by primary intention
(b) diapedesis follows epiboly
(c) chalones control growth inhibition
(d) angiogenic factors are released in the first 24 hours
(e) healing is quicker when Langer's lines are followed

4 Wound dehiscence:

(a) is preceded by a serosanguinous discharge
(b) is commoner in patients on non steroidal anti inflammatory drugs
(c) is caused by poor surgical technique
(d) in the abdomen carries up to 46% mortality
(e) is complicated by incisional hernia in up to 25%

5 The ideal dressing:

(a) is absorbent
(b) allows fluid to escape
(c) is odourless
(d) controls local temperature
(e) is an alginate

3 (a) T
(b) F
(c) T
(d) F
(e) F

Wound healing occurs by primary or secondary intention depending on the size of the wound defect, the cell type (labile, permanent or stable) and the tissue architecture. Local factors (eg infection) and systemic factors (eg steroid use, malnutrition) determine the rate and success of healing. Local mediators for cell migration (epiboly) include cytokines and the reduction in inhibitory factors (chalones). The vascularity of the granulation tissue is stimulated by angiogenesis factors.

4 (a) T
(b) F
(c) T
(d) T
(e) T

The prevention of wound infection by antibiotics and the improvement of surgical technique has made dehiscence uncommon. In the early stages the deeper layers of the wound have opened and this is manifest by the 'pink sign' serosanguinous discharge. If the skin sutures come apart this leads to a 'burst abdomen' and requires the application of a moist warm pack and immediate return to theatre for closure with the use of deep tension sutures. If the skin sutures remain intact an incisional hernia develops.

5 (a) T
(b) F
(c) T
(d) T
(e) F

Wound dressings may be grouped into the hydrocolloid, alginate or occlusive types. The choice is determined by the need for temperature or moisture control, and leak proofing to prevent strike through. Other factors that vary between different types are the degree of allergy, ease of removal, odour, absorbency and the trauma of removal.

UNIT 2 FLUID BALANCE

1 The average daily water balance in a healthy adult in a temperate climate includes:

(a) an intake of 1,000 mls of water from solid food

(b) 150 mls from oxidation

(c) a loss of 400 mls from expired air

(d) a loss of at least 600 mls from insensible cutaneous losses

(e) a faecal loss of 350 mls

2 Metabolic alkalosis:

(a) may be caused by Cushing's Syndrome

(b) may produce Cheyne-Stroke's respiration

(c) produces renal epithelial damage

(d) produces intracellular alkalosis

(e) may be caused by uretero-sigmoidostomy

1 (a) T
(b) F
(c) T
(d) T
(e) F

Water intake is derived from solid food which accounts for 1,000 ml per day and beverages which account for 1,200 mls per day. Water produced from oxidation accounts for approximately 300 mls per day. Water loss includes 1500 ml of urine output, approximately 1,000 mls of insensible loss from the skin and lungs and a further 100 mls in the faeces.

2 (a) T
(b) T
(c) T
(d) F
(e) F

Metabolic alkalosis is characterised by a primary increase in the plasma bicarbonate concentration with a consequent decrease in hydrogen ion concentration. By definition it is caused by a non-respiratory cause and often persists after the primary cause is removed. The cause may be due to loss of unbuffered hydrogen ion which can be of gastrointestinal origin eg gastric aspiration, vomiting with pyloric stenosis, or chloride losing diarrhoea. The renal causes of hydrogen ion loss include mineralocorticoid excess (eg Cushing's syndrome and Conn's syndrome), potassium depletion and drugs with mineralocorticoid activity (eg carbonoxalone). Alkalosis may cause secondary renal injury.

3 The indications for pulmonary artery catheterisation are:

(a) ventricular aneurysm

(b) ischaemia related subaortic valve stenosis

(c) surgery for dissecting abdominal aneurysm

(d) severe pulmonary disease

(e) frequent arterial blood sampling

4 The assessment of the malnourished patient:

(a) does not include dynamometric studies

(b) may involve a lymphocyte count

(c) includes serum transferrin assays

(d) reveals a positive Candida skin test

(e) is confirmed by a body mass index of 25

5 The daily nutritional requirements in a 70 kg man are:

(a) 4 g/kg of nitrogen

(b) 90 mg of Vitamin C per day

(c) half a litre of normal saline to satisfy the Na^+ requirements

(d) increased by 61% in head injured patients

(e) increased by aspirin

3 (a) T
(b) T
(c) T
(d) T
(e) F

The indications for the insertion of a pulmonary artery catheter include established or anticipated left ventricular dysfunction (eg valvular heart disease, ventricular aneurysm, recent myocardial infarction etc), aortic surgery requiring cross clamping of the vessel (eg thoraco-abdominal aortic dissection repair) and severe pulmonary disease (eg pulmonary hypertension, pulmonary emboli).

4 (a) F
(b) T
(c) T
(d) F
(e) F

The assessment of patients who require nutritional support involves a dietary history and clinical examination including height and weight for calculation of the Body Mass Index (normal range is 20–24.9). Special investigations available are biochemical (albumin and transferrin), immunological (delayed type sensitivity), anthopometric (triceps skin fold thickness) and dynamometric (hand grip strength).

5 (a) F
(b) F
(c) T
(d) T
(e) T

The daily nutritional requirements of a 70 kg man include 14 g of nitrogen, 70 mmol of sodium per day and 50 mg of Vitamin C per day. Certain clinical conditions require nutritional supplementation eg sepsis, ileus, pancreatitis, ulcerative colitis, multiple trauma, renal failure and liver disease. Drugs such as aspirin may also increase requirements.

UNIT 3 BLOOD

1 The prothrombin time is prolonged in:

(a) haemophilia
(b) haemolytic jaundice
(c) Vitamin K deficiency
(d) gall stones obstructing the common bile duct
(e) patients given heparin

2 Complications of blood transfusions include:

(a) refractory platelet function
(b) urticaria
(c) fat embolus
(d) brucellosis
(e) immunosuppression

3 Macrocytic anaemia follows:

(a) radical gastrectomy
(b) jejunal diverticulae
(c) Crohn's disease
(d) pregnancy
(e) anticonvulsant therapy

1 (a) F
(b) F
(c) T
(d) T
(e) F

The prothrombin time measures the extrinsic pathway of coagulation, involving factors VII and X, but not factor VIII which is responsible for haemophilia. The Vitamin K dependent factors, III, V, VII, IX and X prolong the PT if deficient. Diseases affecting liver function such as cholestasis will also interfere with the coagulation cascade. Clotting may also be affected by drugs such as heparin and warfarin. Warfarin is a Vitamin K antagonist whilst heparin increases complex formation between antithrombin III and activated serum protease factors (thrombin, XIIa, XIa, Xa, IXa, VIIa).

2 (a) T
(b) T
(c) F
(d) T
(e) T

Other systemic complications are anaphylaxis, volume overload, hypothermia, hyperkalaemia, acidosis, transmission of hepatitis, and HIV. Anaphylaxis is invariably due to a clerical error and leads to a transfusion of incompatible blood. The transfusion service in the United Kingdom has eliminated the risk of transmission of Treponema pallidum and Brucellosis. In addition the blood is screened for HIV and viral hepatitis.

3 (a) T
(b) F
(c) T
(d) T
(e) T

Macrocytic anaemia is the result of Vitamin B12 deficiency. Malabsorption of this vitamin follows total gastrectomy due to the loss of intrinsic factor. Deficiency of B12 may also be due to impaired absorption of the vitamin in the terminal ileum eg Crohn's disease. The requirements increase during pregnancy.

4 The following statements regarding plasma substitutes are true:

(a) Gelofusine and Haemaccel are physiologically the closest to plasma

(b) Hartmann's solution contains 5 mmol/l of potassium

(c) 5% dextrose solution contains no sodium

(d) Cell Saver techniques are passive reinfusions of lost blood

(e) normal saline has a pH of 8

5 Disseminated intravascular coagulation:

(a) platelet fibrin thrombi cause end organ ischaemia

(b) blood is found in the sputum

(c) follows massive blood transfusion

(d) requires anti-coagulation

(e) is associated with subarachnoid haemorrhage

4 (a) F
(b) T
(c) T
(d) F
(e) F

The fluid replacement that most closely resembles plasma is Hartmann's solution. Gelofusine and Haemaccel are colloids which lack electrolytes. 5% dextrose is an isotonic fluid replacement containing water and an isomer of glucose. Blood salvage involves low pressure aspiration followed by filtration or centrifugation prior to reinfusion into the patient. It is suitable in operations where large blood volumes may be lost in the absence of faecal contamination or malignancy eg cardiac surgery, hepatic surgery.

5 (a) T
(b) F
(c) T
(d) F
(e) T

DIC is the inappropriate activation of coagulation with the production of platelet-fibrin thrombi, fibrin degradation products and depletion of coagulation factors. The complications of haemorrhage and end-organ ischaemia requires immediate supportative measures. Subarachnoid haemorrhage, retroperitoneal haemorrhage and renal failure are associated complications. Management requires replacement of coagulation factors, organ support and treatment of the underlying cause in the intensive care setting.

UNIT 4 POST-OPERATIVE COMPLICATIONS

1 Pyrexia is caused by:

(a) deep venous thrombosis

(b) wound infection 24 hours after surgery

(c) gastro intestinal anastomotic leak

(d) phenothiazines

(e) the acute ishcaemic limb

2 Complications of salivary gland surgery include:

(a) great auricular nerve neuroma

(b) gustatory sweating

(c) contralateral gland hyperplasia

(d) submental nerve neurotmesis

(e) cutaneous fistulae

3 Indications for ventilatory support are:

(a) flail chest

(b) elevated intra cranial pressure

(c) a carbon dioxide partial pressure of 8 Kpa

(d) spinal cord injury at the level of the hyoid bone

(e) laparoscopic surgery

1 (a) T
(b) F
(c) T
(d) T
(e) T

The causes of post-operative pyrexia include basal atelectasis, blood transfusion reactions, deep venous thrombosis, pulmonary embolism and chest infections. post-operative pyrexia due to wound infection rarely occurs before 3 days.

2 (a) T
(b) T
(c) F
(d) F
(e) T

Complications of salivary gland surgery are reactionary haemorrhage, especially where hypotensive anaesthesia is used. In the mastoid region the skin flap may slough. A persistent parotid duct fistula may occur or there may be a minor leak of saliva through the wound for several days post-operatively. Facial nerve damage invariably follows formal parotidectomy with recovery time in the order of 2 months, but may be as long as 2 years. Frey's syndrome is the presence of perspiration of the cheek during a meal (gustatory sweating) and may follow parotidectomy. Some advocate the avulsion of the great auricular nerve and tympanic neurectomy as a treatment for Frey's syndrome.

3 (a) T
(b) T
(c) T
(d) T
(e) T

Ventilatory support may be required in both ventilatory ie hypercapnic or hypoxaemic respiratory failure of any cause. A flail chest leads to paradoxical chest movements and therefore ventilatory failure but at a second stage may be associated with ARDS. Intercostal nerve paralysis and/or phrenic nerve injury as well as splinting of the diaphragm as in laparoscopic surgery may also require artificial ventilation.

4 The following statements are true:

(a) Uddin filters are indicated in recurrent pulmonary emboli

(b) perforation occurs once in every 1,700 colonoscopies

(c) Jenkins' rule reduces the incidence of burst abdomen

(d) liver failure complicates ileo-jejunal bypass

(e) post-operative mortality is 0.5%

5 Splenectomy is associated with:

(a) lymphocytosis

(b) thrombotic tendency

(c) gastric fistulae

(d) increased osmotic fragility of red blood cells

(e) reduced Ivy time

4 (a) T
(b) T
(c) T
(d) T
(e) F

Caval filters are indicated in patients with recurrent pulmonary emboli and may be used to prevent PEs in pregnant women with deep venous thromboses. The most frequent complications of colonoscopy are those associated with sedation. Jenkin's rule is a guide in the closure of abdominal wounds and states that the length of suture should be 4 times the length of the wound. By-pass of the jejunum may be used in the management of morbid obesity but carries an operative mortality of 4% and a further mortality at a later date of approximately 6% secondary to hepatic failure due to disturbances in the entero-hepatic circulation and colonisation of the small bowel with bacteria. Micronodular cirrhosis occurs in 9% of patients. The National Confidential Enquiry into Peri-operative Deaths (NCEPOD) devised by Buck, Devlin and Lunn reported a 0.7% 30 day mortality in the 500,000 operations considered in their study.

5 (a) F
(b) T
(c) T
(d) F
(e) F

The complications of splenectomy include thrombocythaemia which may be treated with aspirin when greater than 1 million. Injury to the stomach during ligation of the short gastric vessels may occur with formation of a gastric fistula. Damage to the tail of the pancreas may produce a pancreatic fistula.

UNIT 5 POST-OPERATIVE SEQUELAE

1 In the metabolic response to trauma:

(a) cortisol increases platelet adhesiveness

(b) growth hormone is secreted

(c) Magnesium is conserved

(d) peripheral vascular resistance is reduced

(e) fat restoration is inevitable

2 Immunosuppression:

(a) may present with acalculous cholecystitis

(b) facilitates donor malignancy

(c) decreases colorectal cancer recurrence

(d) is achieved by OKT 3

(e) is associated with lobular carcinoma of the breast

3 Transplantation:

(a) the Terasaki plate assesses compatibility of white cells

(b) Cyclosporin A inhibits the release of interleukin 2

(c) 1 year survival of heart transplantation is 65%

(d) diabetes contraindicates kidney donation

(e) lymphocoele is an early complication

1 (a) T
(b) T
(c) F
(d) F
(e) F

The metabolic response to trauma has three phases: ebb, flow and necrobiosis. The ebb phase is associated with an increase of sympathetic activity which increases the plasma glucose and non esterified fatty acids. There is also an increase in ACTH which increases the plasma cortisol and may increase the adhesive tendency of circulating platelets. If the resuscitation and homeostasis are overwhelmed then necrobiosis ensues, fat is therefore not always restored.

2 (a) T
(b) T
(c) F
(d) T
(e) F

Acalculous cholecystitis tends to affect the immunocompromised and diabetics. The lack of a viable immune response increases the risk of successful implantation and proliferation of neoplastic cells. It has also been inferred that the immunosuppression induced by large blood transfusions may increase the risk of recurrence of colo-rectal malignancy. OKT 3 is one of the substances used in the treatment of steroid resistant acute rejection.

3 (a) T
(b) T
(c) F
(d) F
(e) T

Tissue typing has the aim of reducing the incidence of rejection. This is achieved by a microtoxicity assay using antisera against MHC antigens on Terasaki plates. Immunosuppression is achieved by a combination of steroids (reduction of IL1), azathioprine (reduced replication of T helper cells) and cyclosporin reduction of IL2).

4 Pain pathways:

(a) the substantia gelatinosa controls the passage of pain impulse

(b) Melzack and Wall described the Pattern theory of pain

(c) 'wind up' produces chronic pain

(d) C fibres are myelinated fast fibres

(e) paracetamol acts centrally

5 Post-operative pain control:

(a) mid line incisions are less painful than transverse

(b) analgesia reduces the incidence of myocardial infarction

(c) may be achieved by a Biers block

(d) includes the use of physiotherapy

(e) infiltration of bupivacaine reduces systemic analgesic requirements

4 (a) T
(b) F
(c) T
(d) F
(e) T

Pain is a subjective unpleasant experience perceived in the cerebral cortex. The modulation theory (gate theory) of Melzack and Wall suggests that there is a control mechanism in the substantia gelatinosa which acts as a gate. The implication is that impulses carried by C fibres can be blocked by the arrival of faster A fibres or other impulses that descend from the brain by this gate mechanism. This is the explanation for 'combat analgesia' experienced by soldiers in battle.

5 (a) F
(b) T
(c) F
(d) F
(e) T

Post-operative pain should be prevented and treated because it is humanitarian, reduces morbidity, reduces hospital stay and is cost efficient. The Joint College Report (1990) states that the treatment of pain after surgery in British Hospitals has been inadequate. Post-operative pain control should be pre-emptive wherever possible, including wound infiltration with bupivacaine and patient controlled analgesia.

CORE MODULE 3

Trauma

UNIT 1 INITIAL ASSESSMENT AND RESUSCITATION AFTER TRAUMA

1 The Primary Survey of a multiply injured patient:

(a) there is no direct correlation between the time required for initial assessment and resuscitation and long term survival

(b) requires the Glasgow Coma Scale to assess the level of consciousness

(c) a log roll is performed to identify spinal injury

(d) failed endotracheal intubation warrants needle cricothyroidotomy

(e) shock is absent in the presence of a heart rate of 72 bpm

2 The following may be a part of primary resuscitation:

(a) central venous catheterisation

(b) chest drainage

(c) pericardiocentesis

(d) urethral catheterisation

(e) relief of caval compression in pregnant women

1 (a) F
(b) F
(c) F
(d) T
(e) F

The aim of Primary Survey is the diagnosis and initial treatment of life threatening problems. The time required to resuscitate a trauma patient correlates well with the long term outcome of these patients. The neurological assessment in the Primary Survey is more basic than the GCS, the key aspects being whether the patient is Alert, responds to Verbal or Painful stimuli or is Unresponsive (AVPU). The log rolling of the patient is part of the secondary survey which is a head to toe examination of the injured patient. In the hierarchy of airway management if an experienced practitioner is unable to intubate the patient a surgical airway is required. The pulse in a fit young patient may remain unaltered until considerable blood loss occurs.

2 (a) F
(b) F
(c) T
(d) F
(e) T

By the end of the Primary Survey life threatening conditions have been diagnosed and treated, venous access is established, basic blood investigations have been requested, the patient is being monitored, urinary catheter and NG tube are in situ if required and the essential trauma radiographs (C spine, chest and pelvis) have been performed. Pregnant women in shock following trauma should be placed on their left side to avoid compression of the inferior vena cava.

3 Upper airway obstruction in the casualty department requires:

(a) extension of the neck

(b) naso-pharyngeal intubation

(c) the Heimlich manoeuvre

(d) finger sweep

(e) ventilation

4 In Baskett's classification (1991) of shock:

(a) septicaemia is described as warm shock

(b) loss of 3 litres of blood is grade 4

(c) there is no change in respiratory rate following loss of 25% of blood volume

(d) pulse pressure is increased in stage 3

(e) capillary refill is normal until at least 15% of blood volume is lost

5 In tension pneumothorax:

(a) an urgent chest X-ray is requested

(b) a 14 gauge cannula is inserted in the anterior axillary line

(c) the mediastinum is displaced away from the affected side

(d) breath sounds are increased

(e) an underwater sealed chest drain is held at body level

3 (a) F
(b) T
(c) F
(d) T
(e) F

If the airway is obstructed the mouth should be opened and foreign material or loose teeth are removed by finger sweep or suction. The neck is kept straight and in line and a jaw thrust manouvre is performed. 100% oxygen is given. If ventilation is still not possible and oro-pharyngeal airway is unsuccessful, the patient is intubated by the oral or nasal route.

4 (a) F
(b) T
(c) F
(d) F
(e) T

Baskett's classified hypovolaemic shock into 4 grades. Grade 1 implies a blood loss < 0.75 litres (15% blood volume) with a pulse < 100, normal capillary refill, respiratory rate and urine output etc. Blood loss > 2 litres is grade 4 shock and carries a poor prognosis. The respiratory rate begins to rise in grade 3 shock where > 1.5 litres (> 30% blood vol) is lost.

5 (a) F
(b) F
(c) T
(d) F
(e) F

Tension pneumothorax is a clinical diagnosis. The patient becomes increasingly short of breath despite a clear airway. The chest appears hyperexpanded, the neck veins are distended and there is tracheal deviation away from the affected side. The breath sounds may be decreased but in practice the noise of the trauma room makes this an unreliable sign. The treatment of choice is needle thoraco-centesis (2nd intercostal space mid clavicular line) followed by a chest drain.

UNIT 2 CHEST, ABDOMEN AND PELVIS

1 Diagnostic peritoneal lavage:

(a) is indicated in hypotensive intoxicated patients

(b) is positive if red blood cell count is > 100,000 per ml

(c) if positive warrants laparotomy

(d) involves intracoelomic infusion of 500 mls of saline

(e) is performed at McBurney's point

2 45 minutes following traumatic loss of 2 litres of blood:

(a) stroke volume reduces as a result of decreased venous return

(b) the haematocrit has fallen

(c) there is a tendency to anaerobic respiration

(d) atrial natiuretic peptide inhibition is the most potent anti-diuretic

(e) a reflex vasoconstriction is accompanied by venous collapse

1 (a) T
(b) T
(c) T
(d) F
(e) F

Diagnostic peritoneal lavage is indicated in cases of suspected abdominal trauma where a depressed level of consciousness or an altered pain response may lead to a false negative physical examination. Other circumstances where it may be used are where the abdominal findings are equivocal bearing in mind that over half of all patients with significant intra-abdominal injury will not have positive abdominal findings at presentation. 1 litre of saline is infused into the abdominal cavity immediately above or below the umbilicus and then siphoned out of the pelvis. The procedure is ideally performed by the surgeon who would perform the laparotomy given that a positive result is an indication for surgery.

2 (a) T
(b) F
(c) T
(d) F
(e) T

Blood loss following trauma of > 30% is manifest by a tachycardia and a fall in blood pressure. To maintain cardiac output the heart rate increases to compensate for the reduced stroke volume. There is also a peripheral vasoconstriction. The shift in fluids from extravascular compartments into the circulation aids in the compensation of hypovolaemia, however the haematocrit does not change for at least 1 hour. The circulation preferentially supports the brain and heart with resultant increased anaerobic respiration and lactic acidosis in the peripheries. Anti diuretic hormone and aldosterone are the most potent hormones in the conservation of water.

3 Treatment of a flail chest includes:

(a) intermittent positive ventilation

(b) local anaesthetic injected at the fracture site

(c) surgical intervention if blood loss greater than 1,500 mls

(d) use of Doxapram

(e) prophylactic chest drainage

4 Complications of pelvic fractures are:

(a) perforation of the rectum

(b) aortic rupture

(c) direct inguinal hernias

(d) urethral strictures

(e) impotence

3 (a) T
(b) F
(c) T
(d) F
(e) F

A flail chest occurs when one part of the chest wall ceases to have bony continuity with the rest of the thorax, usually due to multiple rib fractures. This leads to a paradoxical movement of the chest wall. The management of a flail chest requires adequate oxygenation and judicious fluid balance with a view to avoiding over hydration. Mechanical ventilation may be required and analgesia is imperative to allow a good ventilatory effort. The coexistence of a haemothorax of greater than 1,500 mls is an indication for a thoracotomy as is the drainage of greater than 400 mls for 4 consecutive hours.

4 (a) T
(b) F
(c) F
(d) T
(e) T

Pelvic fractures are life threatening. Associated injuries may occur to any of the structures contained within the pelvis. Severe haemorrhage may be due to injury to iliac arteries or veins as well as bleeding from the fracture site itself. The genitals, urethra and bladder are also at risk due to their position. Any of the gastrointestinal structures present within the pelvis may be injured and open fractures with gastrointestinal contamination are best treated with a colostomy. Neurological injury may also occur, most commonly of the sciatic and sacral nerves the latter of which can lead to impotence.

5 Splenic rupture:

(a) may be associated with Kehr's sign

(b) is accompanied by the fracture of the transverse processes of the lumbar spine

(c) is ideally treated with conservation in infants

(d) may present following reactive haemorrhage

(e) produces left flank shifting dullness

5 (a) T
(b) F
(c) T
(d) T
(e) F

Splenic rupture should be suspected in multiply injured patients and in particular those in whom trauma to the left upper quadrant or left lower thorax has occurred. The patient may present shocked or become so after an initial period of recovery that may last days. Apart from the systemic signs of internal haemorrhage (pallor, tachycardia, tachypnoea, restlessness etc) the local signs include left shoulder tip pain (Kehr's sign) which may be elicited by raising the foot of the bed and is due to referred diaphragmatic irritation. Less commonly (25% of cases) shifting dullness may be present in the right flank – Ballance's sign. Splenectomy is avoided where possible due to the risk of overwhelming post-splenectomy sepsis.

UNIT 3 CENTRAL NERVOUS SYSTEM TRAUMA

1 Elevated intracranial pressure:

(a) produces hypertension with bradycardia

(b) reduces venous outflow

(c) leads to an increased CSF production

(d) is associated with tachypnoea

(e) of 10 mmHg requires surgical intervention

2 Indications for admission following head injury are:

(a) blood loss greater than 400 mls

(b) skull fracture

(c) convulsion

(d) age greater than 70 years

(e) post traumatic amnesia

3 In spinal shock:

(a) the blood pressures are low

(b) recovery is characterised by paraplegic flexion

(c) normally lasts between 2 and 7 days

(d) profuse sweating occurs above the level of transection

(e) blood in the CSF is diagnostic

1 (a) T
(b) F
(c) F
(d) F
(e) F

Increased intracranial pressure classically presents with signs of headache, oculomotor palsies, Cushing's reflex/triad (hypertension, bradycardia, respiratory irregularities) and papilloedema. According to the Monro Kelly doctrine the signs will occur once the compensatory evacuation of CSF and venous blood from the rigid skull has occurred. The normal values of ICP are 10–15cm of water and treatment is indicated if values are higher than this.

2 (a) F
(b) T
(c) T
(d) F
(e) F

The indications for admission to hospital following a head injury are depressed or altered level of consciousness, skull fracture, focal neurological signs, persistent vomiting, severe headache, significant coexisting disorders that may further complicate a head injury (eg psychiatric disorders) and social factors.

3 (a) T
(b) T
(c) T
(d) F
(e) F

Spinal shock follows injury to the spine, especially when this is complete. It is due to an abrupt loss of sympathetic tone and is therefore characterised by hypotension and bradycardia. There is flaccid paralysis and loss of sensation. When recovery occurs after some days this is characterised by paraplegic flexion.

4 Lumbar puncture in suspected meningitis:

(a) should be performed urgently in absence of raised intra cranial pressure

(b) must be performed before antibiotics are given

(c) may be normal in early pyogenic meningitis

(d) requires 6 samples of CSF for Gram stain

(e) is an alternative to CT scanning

5 Subarachnoid haemorrhage:

(a) has a mortality of 12% in the presence of neck stiffness and focal neurology

(b) is caused by multiple Berry aneurysm in 35%

(c) is associated with polycystic kidneys

(d) produces xanthochromic CSF

(e) is more reliably diagnosed on arteriography than CT

4 (a) T
(b) F
(c) T
(d) F
(e) F

Lumbar puncture is the key diagnostic test in meningitis. It should be performed immediately if there are no signs of raised intracranial pressure or focal neurological signs. Some prefer to perform an urgent CT before the lumber puncture. However, in the presence of clinical signs of meningitis high dose intravenous benzylpenicillin should be given.

5 (a) T
(b) F
(c) T
(d) T
(e) T

Bleeding into the subarachnoid space is due to aneurysmal rupture in 80% of cases. These are mostly Berry aneurysms which may be of genetic origin – type III collagen deficiencies, polycystic kidneys and Ehlers Danlos syndrome are known associations. The degree of mortality is very much related to the number and severity of symptoms at presentation with 12% mortality in the presence of neck stiffness and focal neurology and a 100% mortality for those presenting with prolonged coma. Computerised tomography and lumber puncture where xanthochromia is present may be diagnostic.

UNIT 4 SPECIAL PROBLEMS

1 Triage:

(a) requires a doctor
(b) was first developed in the battlefield
(c) is the prioritisation of head injured patients
(d) involves Primary and Secondary survey
(e) is performed where casualties exceed medical services

2 High velocity gun injury:

(a) produces narrow tracks due to cavitation
(b) are associated with multiple exit wounds
(c) produce more injury than low velocity
(d) are treated conservatively
(e) produces injury to distant organs

3 Deep dermal burns:

(a) is a partial thickness burn
(b) are anaesthetic
(c) require tetanus prophylaxis
(d) heal by restitution
(e) of the face represent 18% surface area

1 (a) F
(b) T
(c) F
(d) F
(e) T

Triage comes from the French verb 'to sort'. It was developed during wartime by Napoleon's surgeon marshal to manage resources appropriately in the battlefield. It is adopted in cases of trauma where the demand outstrips the facilities and manpower. The triage officer is ideally a senior doctor only in cases of major incidents. In other cases it is sufficient that a trained nurse performs this duty as in accident and emergency departments.

2 (a) F
(b) F
(c) T
(d) F
(e) T

Gunshot injuries produce tissue damage in proportion to the velocity of the bullet and therefore the energy absorbed by the body. Low velocity bullets cause damage along the track which they create. High velocity gunshot wounds are characterised by an explosive pressure and a decompression effect causing widespread tissue damage, even distant from the primary tract.

3 (a) T
(b) F
(c) T
(d) F
(e) F

A deep dermal burn is one that extends deeply into the dermis but enough adnexial tissue remains unharmed to allow spontaneous tissue healing with scar formation. Sensation is preserved. The calculation of fluid replacement requires the knowledge of the approximate percentage area burned. The Rule of Nines is applied and in this the head represents a surface area of 9%.

4 Physiological scoring systems:

(a) include the Revised Trauma Score

(b) require more medical knowledge than anatomical scoring

(c) are used for Triage

(d) are of predictive value for survival

(e) rely on the Cambridge Cruciform

5 Contaminated wounds:

(a) require debridement

(b) are graded by Gustilo and Anderson

(c) are treated with immediate grafting following toilet

(d) are at risk of Clostridial infection

(e) are treated by primary closure

4 (a) T
(b) F
(c) T
(d) T
(e) F

Physiological scoring systems are used to assess the consequences of injury. They are quick and reproducible, require little medical knowledge and are easy to apply. It is a method used when casualties exceed the ability to provide optimal care. The Cambridge cruciform and Thames label are used to indicate the priority rating of the patient.

5 (a) T
(b) F
(c) F
(d) T
(e) F

Contaminated wounds require a toilet-debridement. Gustilo and Anderson classified compound fractures according to the accompanying wound and its degree of contamination. Dirty wounds may harbour Clostridia, spore forming anaerobes rendering tetanus prophylaxis obligatory. Both primary closure and skin grafting are usually ill advised when any risk of contamination persists.

UNIT 5 PRINCIPLES OF LIMB SURGERY

1 Causes of delayed union are:

(a) interposition of soft tissues at the fracture site

(b) osteoporosis

(c) immobilization

(d) intensive antibiotic therapy

(e) steroid therapy

2 Nerve conduction:

(a) is permanently impaired following axonotmesis

(b) recovery takes up to 6 months in neuropraxia

(c) requires myelin

(d) is faster in the presence of Nodes of Ranvier

(e) is unidirectional

3 Compartment syndrome:

(a) may follow reperfusion following vascular trauma

(b) is defined as a compartment pressure that exceeds the diastolic pressure

(c) requires fasciotomy

(d) may be a consequence of external splintage

(e) is also known as Volkmann's ischaemic contracture

1 (a) T
(b) F
(c) T
(d) F
(e) T

Delayed union is the term used to describe a bone that displays abnormal movement when the fracture site is stressed at a time when under normal circumstances one would expect healing to have occurred. The causes are either local or systemic. The systemic factors include age, nutritional status, general health and concurrent medication such as steroids. Local factors include under or excessively rigid immobilisation, poor blood supply, infection or interposition of other tissues.

2 (a) F
(b) T
(c) F
(d) T
(e) T

Nerve conduction is unidirectional and may be carried in either myelinated or unmyelinated fibres. Seddon classified nerve injury from a functional point of view. Neuropraxia is a reversible interruption of nerve conduction without damage to the axon or its supporting cells. Axonotmesis represents an anatomical disruption of the axon with an intact sheath. It is in this sheath that regeneration will occur at a rate that varies according to local and systemic factors.

3 (a) T
(b) F
(c) T
(d) T
(e) T

Compartment syndrome is an increase in pressure within a closed compartment or closed space that leads to ischaemic changes to the contents of the space. It may be caused by either increasing the pressure within a space or decreasing the space itself. A compartment pressure of greater than 30 mmHg less than the diastolic requires fasciotomy – the treatment of choice. Failure to do so leads to Volkmann's ischaemic contracture, which in the limbs presents with irreversible clawing.

4 Fat embolism:

(a) produces end organ ischaemia

(b) may be diagnosed by fat in body fluids

(c) is a feature of liver trauma

(d) reduces the function of platelets

(e) does not cause a ventilation perfusion mismatch

5 Brachial plexus injuries:

(a) Klumpke type injury follows excessive lateral neck flexion

(b) Froment's sign is positive in lower brachial plexus injuries

(c) Erb-Duchenne type injury is characterised by a claw-like hand

(d) may follow central line insertion

(e) when suspected require immediate repair

4 (a) T
(b) T
(c) T
(d) T
(e) F

Fat embolism may follow multiple injuries and fractures. By definition the fat emboli should involve the pulmonary and one other system. The fat was originally thought to be of marrow origin but it may also be due to derangement of fat metabolism. Fat may be present in the sputum or urine but the diagnosis is suspected in multiply injured patients that present respiratory, neurological and other systemic symptoms of organ ischaemia 24 hours or more after major injuries. The syndrome is also characterised by dysfunction of the blood constituents including the red blood cells, the white blood cells and platelets.

5 (a) F
(b) T
(c) F
(d) T
(e) F

Brachial plexus injuries are a more complex form of nerve injury but the principles of sensory, motor, autonomic reflex and trophic effects are the same. The injuries are divided into 2 groups. Upper brachial plexus injuries (Erb-Duchenne), due to displacement of the head with respect to the shoulder leads to the characteristic waiters tip position. Lower brachial plexus injuries (Klumpke) are caused by hyperextension injuries of the arm, are less common and lead to a claw-like hand. The more proximal the injury the worse the prognosis. Repair is indicated in those cases that are more distal and do not respond to conservative therapy.

CORE MODULE 4

Intensive care

UNIT 1 CARDIOVASCULAR

1 Cardiac output is increased by:

(a) endotoxaemia and shock

(b) hypervolaemia

(c) pneumothorax

(d) sympathetic stimulation

(e) altitude

2 Systemic circulation vasodilators include:

(a) calcium channel blockers

(b) ischaemia

(c) carbon dioxide

(d) glyceryl trinitrate

(e) prostaglandin E2

1 (a) T
(b) F
(c) F
(d) T
(e) T

Cardiac output is a product of the stroke volume and the heart rate. Endotoxic shock is a high output shock, also known as warm shock. The cause of the shock is peripheral vasodilatation to which the heart responds by increasing the cardiac output. Excess volume may lead to cardiac failure in those predisposed – see Starlings law and curve. A pneumothorax leads to a reduced venous return due to a reduced negative intrathoracic pressure, this in turn reduces the cardiac output. Sympathetic stimulation increases the heart rate. An increased cardiac output in the non acclimatized is a compensatory measure for reduced partial pressure of oxygen at altitude.

2 (a) T
(b) T
(c) T
(d) T
(e) T

Carbon dioxide and ischaemia are physiological vasodilators that act as a protective mechanism against tissue damage. Calcium channel blockers and GTN both vasodilate vessels and in doing so increase cardiac perfusion and decrease after-load. Some prostaglandins regulate blood flow locally.

3 In a cardiac arrest:

(a) the patient should be given 10 mls 1:1,000 adrenaline if in asystole

(b) defibrillation with 200 joules is repeated 3 times initially

(c) tension pneumothorax may be responsible

(d) 200 mg of lignocaine may be given via the endotracheal tube

(e) radial pulse should be monitored by team leader

4 Cardiac tamponade:

(a) Beck's triad is present

(b) if suspected thoracotomy is indicated

(c) is a cause of VF arrest

(d) may be caused by Dressler's syndrome following cardiac surgery

(e) is treated with pericardiectomy if chronic

5 Complications of central venous catheterisation include:

(a) claw-like hand

(b) tension pneumothorax

(c) chylothorax

(d) Horner's syndrome

(e) recurrent laryngeal nerve palsy

3 (a) F
(b) F
(c) T
(d) T
(e) F

Cardiac arrest protocols are required to be known by the surgical trainee, you may be the most senior person at an arrest. In asystole 1 mg of adrenaline may be given, this is equivalent to 10 mls of 1:10,000. The patient is given two 200 j shocks before proceeding to a larger 360 j shock. Tension pneumothorax may lead to electro-mechanical dissociation and must be excluded along with cardiac tamponade, hypovolaemia, hypothermia and a massive pulmonary embolus. The team leader coordinates activity during a cardiac arrest and monitors a large artery such as the femoral artery, small arteries may be difficult to feel.

4 (a) T
(b) F
(c) F
(d) T
(e) T

The signs that characterise a cardiac tamponade are muffled heart sounds, hypotension and distended neck veins. These constitute Beck's triad. Cardiac tamponade causes a cardiac arrest by electro-mechanical dissociation. Dressler's syndrome is a post myocardial infarction syndrome that follows weeks after an infarction or cardiac surgery and may be associated with a tamponade.

5 (a) T
(b) F
(c) T
(d) T
(e) F

Central venous catheterisation via a subclavian route can injure the brachial plexus leading to a claw-like hand when C8 and T1 are affected. Simple pneumothorax is the complication that can occur if the pleural space is entered. Equally if the thoracic duct or stellate ganglion are injured it may lead to a chylothorax and a Horner's syndrome respectively.

UNIT 2 RESPIRATORY

1 Adult respiratory distress syndrome:

(a) is manifest by hypoxaemia responsive only to 100% oxygen therapy

(b) is associated with excess surfactant

(c) decreases the elasticity of the lung

(d) is also known as shock lung

(e) treatment includes steroid therapy

2 In a healthy 70 kg male patient:

(a) perfusion is approximately 80% of alveolar ventilation

(b) FEV_1 is greater than 70% of forced vital capacity

(c) tidal volume is half a litre

(d) dead space is negligible

(e) Fi O_2 is 25%

3 Intermittent Positive Pressure Ventilation:

(a) increases dead space

(b) increases preload

(c) increases pressure within the pleural space

(d) requires muscle paralysis

(e) may not be given via a tracheostomy tube

1 (a) F
(b) F
(c) T
(d) T
(e) T

Adult respiratory distress syndrome, formerly known as shock lung is a form of respiratory failure not responsive to oxygen therapy. It is characterised by decreased lung compliance and there is less surfactant within the alveoli. The patients benefit from ventilation and steroids may be beneficial.

2 (a) F
(b) T
(c) T
(d) F
(e) F

Normally perfusion and ventilation have a 1:1 ratio. The forced expiration volume in the first second should be greater than 80%. The tidal volume – a normal breath – is 500 mls and includes 150 mls of dead space. The atmospheric oxygen concentration is 21%.

3 (a) F
(b) T
(c) T
(d) T
(e) F

IPPV will decrease the dead space because it entails endotracheal intubation or a tracheostomy. By decreasing intrathoracic pressure the venous return increases hence increasing the cardiac preload.

4 Early respiratory complications of surgery:

(a) are characterised by absence of pyrexia

(b) may lead to ECG changes

(c) may require mini-tracheostomy

(d) include pneumothorax

(e) are reduced by prophylactic antibiotics

5 The following are causes of respiratory failure.

(a) low cervical spine fracture

(b) myasthaenia gravis

(c) multiple rib fractures

(d) fat embolism

(e) barotrauma

4 (a) F
(b) T
(c) T
(d) T
(e) F

Pyrexia may accompany basal atellectasis as well as pulmonary emboli. Pulmonary embolism may be associated with characteristic ECG changes. Mucous plugs and atellectasis require respiratory physiotherapy and may also require suction via a surgical airway. Prophylactic antibiotics serve to reduce wound infection and do not reduce the incidence of basal atellectasis.

5 (a) F
(b) T
(c) T
(d) T
(e) T

Causes of respiratory failure may be classified as a failure of central drive (opiate overdose), neural pathways (high cervical spine fracture), neuromuscular transmission, muscle power (muscular dystrophy), mechanical support of the lungs (pneumothorax), lung parenchyma (interstitial infiltrates), alveoli (oedema), airways (asthma), and pulmonary blood supply (emboli).

UNIT 3 MULTISYSTEM FAILURE

1 In acute pancreatitis:

(a) amylase is a marker of severity
(b) mortality is > 95% in multisystem failure
(c) presence of pleural effusion indicates severity
(d) oxygen free radicals contribute to microvasular damage
(e) nitrous oxide synthetase increases peripheral resistance

2 Pre-renal failure:

(a) is the second commonest cause of renal failure in surgical patients
(b) is a manifestation of poor cardiac output
(c) responds to frusemide infusion following adequate filling
(d) may be caused by retroperitoneal fibrosis
(e) leads to acidosis

3 Systemic inflammatory response syndrome criteria include:

(a) temperature < 36°C
(b) heart rate > 120 bpm
(c) respiratory rate > 20 breaths per minute
(d) C reactive protein > 5
(e) haemoglobin < 9 g/dl

1 (a) F
(b) T
(c) T
(d) T
(e) F

Inability to identify severe acute pancreatitis increases the morbidity of this life threatening condition. Various severity score systems have been devised; the most widely used in the UK is the Glasgow/Ranson criteria. The presence of 3 or more criteria or of a systemic complication eg pleural effusion indicates severity.

2 (a) F
(b) T
(c) T
(d) F
(e) T

Pre-renal failure secondary to hypovolaemia is the commonest surgical cause of renal failure. Equally hypoperfusion of the kidneys may be due to cardiac failure. Low dose frusemide or dopamine may be used with success to maintain diuresis. Retroperitoneal fibrosis which is most commonly idiopathic may obstruct the urinary tract leading to post renal failure. The ability of the kidney to excrete the acids produced by the body's metabolic processes is essential for acid base balance.

3 (a) T
(b) F
(c) T
(d) F
(e) F

Systemic inflammatory response syndrome is related to the degree of inflammatory response and is associated with infectious and non infectious insults such as trauma, pancreatitis and surgery. Four criteria are used: temperature, heart rate, respiratory rate and white cell count. A more severe inflammatory response is detrimental and is associated with multiple organ dysfunction syndrome.

4 Mediators of multisystem failure:

(a) tumour necrosis factor enhaces muscle breakdown into amino acids

(b) interleukin 6 induces fever

(c) platelet activating factor causes vasodilatation

(d) interleukin 1 activates neutrophils and macrophages

(e) circulating interleukin 1 levels inversely correlates with severity

5 Indications for Total Parenteral Nutrition are:

(a) carcinomatosis peritonei

(b) mesenteric ischaemia

(c) basal skull fracture

(d) less than 90 cm of small bowel

(e) necrotising pancreatitis

4 (a) T
(b) F
(c) T
(d) T
(e) F

Tumour necrosis factor induces fever and anorexia, encourages muscle breakdown to amino acids, increases neutrophil margination, activates monocytes and macrophages and induces other mediators. Interleukin 6 enhances B cell activity and increases acute phase protein synthesis – interleukin 1 induces fever. Platelet activating factor is a vasoactive lipid produced by the cells of inflammation in sepsis. Apart from being a pyrogen interleukin 1 also activates neutrophils and macrophages and activates the mediator cascade.

5 (a) F
(b) T
(c) F
(d) T
(e) T

Total parenteral nutrition is given to those patients requiring nutritional support in whom the gastrointestinal tract is temporarily or permanently non functioning. The indications are determined by the history, examination and special investigations. The indications are obvious severe malnutrition (> 10% weight loss, serum albumin < 30 g/l, gross muscle wasting); moderate malnutrition (poor dietary history for at least 4 weeks with no physical evidence of malnutrition); normal or near normal nutritional status with an underlying pathology that is likely to result in malnutrition (burns, multiple injury).

UNIT 4 PROBLEMS IN INTENSIVE CARE

1 The following statements regarding sepsis are true:

(a) S aureus is present in the nostrils of 50% of the population

(b) S epidermidis is responsible for osteomyelitis

(c) S pyogenes is spread by contact

(d) S faecalis is responsible for abdominal sepsis

(e) S saprophyticus is responsible for urinary infections in the elderly

2 Regarding Clostridia:

(a) C tetani may cause Pseudomembranous Colitis

(b) C perfringens may complicate open crush injury

(c) C difficle is sensitive to oral metronidazol

(d) Clostridia are spore forming aerobes

(e) C difficle is found in carnivorous urinary tract

3 Complications of thoracic surgery include:

(a) chylothorax

(b) Erb-Duchenne palsy

(c) Horner's syndrome

(d) fat embolus

(e) tracheo-oesophageal fistula

1 (a) T
(b) F
(c) T
(d) T
(e) T

Staphylococcus aureus exists in the nose and on the moist skin of healthy people and may lead to opportunistic infection such as carbuncles and osteomyelitis when mucosae or the skin are damaged. Streptococci are gram positive spherical bacteria that multiply to form chains of organisms. S pyogenes is haemolytic and the majority that cause adult human infection are Lancefield group A and spread by direct contact. Faecal streptococci frequently cause urinary tract infection and biliary infection.

2 (a) F
(b) T
(c) T
(d) F
(e) F

Clostridia are spore forming Gram positive obligate anaerobes. Clostridium difficile is responsible for pseudomembranous colitis that may follow antibiotic therapy particularly in the elderly. It may be treated with metronidazole. Clostridium perfringens is the most frequently encountered organism in gas gangrene and may follow crush injury where tissue anoxia favours growth.

3 (a) T
(b) F
(c) T
(d) F
(e) T

Lymphatic leakage may follow damage to the thoracic duct. Horner's syndrome may follow damage to the stellate ganglion. One of the acquired causes of tracheo-oesophageal fistulae are leaks from oesophageal anastomoses.

4 The following statements regarding oliguria are true:

(a) oliguria is defined as a urine output of < 0.5 ml/kg/min

(b) the first line of treatment is the administration of 20 mg of Frusemide IV

(c) if urine osmolality is twice that of plasma then renal failure is present

(d) metabolic acidosis is identified by blood gas measurements

(e) serum potassium falls in renal failure

5 The complications of a lung abscess are:

(a) cerebral abscess formation

(b) reactive haemorrhage

(c) empyema

(d) axillary vein thrombosis

(e) bilateral hilar infiltrates

4 (a) T
(b) F
(c) F
(d) T
(e) F

Renal failure is a frequent event in Intensive Care Units. The commonest cause in surgical patients is hypoperfusion of the kidneys. Acute renal failure presents as oliguria. Other causes of oliguria (blocked urinary catheter, sodium and water retention due to the stress response etc) should be excluded. Immediate management following correction of hypovolaemia includes dopamine infusion, fluid restriction to 20 ml/hr plus the previous hour's urine output and regular urea, electrolytes and creatinine measurements. Blood gas analysis are essential to identify acid-base derangement.

5 (a) T
(b) F
(c) T
(d) F
(e) F

Lung abscesses are the commonest cause of secondary cerebral abscesses. Lung abscesses may lead to secondary haemorrhage due to erosion of the abscess into blood vessels. Bilateral hilar infiltrates are characteristic of ARDS which is not associated with lung abscess formation.

UNIT 5 PRINCIPLES OF THE INTENSIVE CARE UNIT

1 Indications for admission:

(a) haemodialysis

(b) frequent medical intervention

(c) continuous positive pressure ventilation

(d) invasive arterial pressure monitoring

(e) heavy nursing requirement

2 Methods of monitoring used in the intensive care unit include:

(a) end tidal CO_2

(b) ventilatory minute volume

(c) lactic dehydrogenase to indicate severity of trauma

(d) pulmonary capillary wedge pressure

(e) diagnostic peritoneal lavage

3 Indications for renal support include:

(a) potassium greater than 6.5 mmol/l

(b) oliguria responsive to fluid challenge

(c) acidaemia

(d) lemon yellow tinge

(e) creatinine greater than 145 mmol/l

1 (a) F
(b) T
(c) T
(d) T
(e) T

The indications for admission to an intensive care unit may be summarised into 4 groups: organ support (respiratory, cardiac etc), invasive monitoring, frequent medical intervention and heavy nursing. Though renal failure patients may be admitted for haemofiltration, haemodialysis is performed on an out-patient basis.

2 (a) T
(b) T
(c) T
(d) T
(e) F

Monitoring of vital functions is one of the indications for admission to the Intensive Care Unit. Respiratory function is monitored by measuring the arterial oxygen saturation with a pulse oximeter, arterial blood gas analysis, ventilatory minute volume and end-tidal carbon dioxide analysis. Measurement of the end-tidal carbon dioxide indicates the arterial carbon dioxide tension since alveolar and arterial carbon dioxide tensions are closely matched. Central venous pressure measurement is replaced by Swann-Ganz catherisation when cardiac filling of the right and left ventricles is presumed to be equal. When left ventricular ischaemia or valve disease is present the left atrial pressure is measured by placement of a balloon tipped pulmonary artery catheter.

3 (a) T
(b) F
(c) T
(d) F
(e) F

The indications for renal dialysis are Hyperkalaemia > 6.5 mmol/l, fluid overload, metabolic acidosis and uraemia > 50 mmol/l.

4 The following are prognostic scoring systems:

(a) the Glasgow criteria

(b) APACHE

(c) ASA

(d) Weber

(e) Le Fort

5 The requirements of an intensive care unit are:

(a) a minimum of 0.5% of all inpatient beds

(b) a 1 patient to 1 nurse ratio

(c) 30 m^2 area per bed

(d) good ventilation with open windows

(e) not more than 15 minutes from the Accident and Emergency Department

4 (a) T
(b) T
(c) F
(d) F
(e) F

The Glasgow criteria are used to assess the severity of acute pancreatitis. APACHE II is a scoring system used in intensive care units designed to predict mortality in critically ill patients. The American Society of Anaesthetists scoring system of pre-operative status is not designed to be a predictor of outcome but to be a facilitator of communication between clinicians. It does however correlate well with total operative mortality. Weber is a classification system for ankle fractures and Le Fort famously classified facial fractures anatomically.

5 (a) F
(b) T
(c) F
(d) F
(e) F

The department of health recommends that 1% of acute hospital beds are allocated to ICU. The nursing input requires a 1:1 ratio of patients to nurses. At least 20 m^2 of space are required for each bed to allow safe monitoring and procedures to be carried out. The environment should be air conditioned. The ICU should be located close to the operating theatre, but the distance from the Accident and Emergency Department is not a key factor.

CORE MODULE 5

Neoplasia, techniques and outcome of surgery

UNIT 1 PRINCIPLES OF ONCOLOGY

1 The following are techniques used in cancer surgery:

(a) spinal decompression

(b) prosthetic bone replacement

(c) staging laparoscopy in non Hodgkins lymphoma

(d) amputation for pain

(e) adrenalectomy in breast cancer

2 Staging:

(a) is a measure of tumour load

(b) is not a prognostic indicator in lung cancer

(c) considers nuclear pleomorphism

(d) routinely includes bone scanning in breast cancer

(e) may include tumour markers

1 (a) T
(b) T
(c) F
(d) T
(e) T

The surgeon's involvement in malignant disease may be diagnostic (biopsy), curative (removal of all macroscopic tumour and regional lymph node drainage), palliative (for pain, alleviation of obstruction and reduction of transfusion requirements) or reconstructive (for function or aesthetics). Staging splenectomy and adrenalectomy have been all but replaced by CT scanning and hormonal manipulation respectively.

2 (a) T
(b) F
(c) F
(d) T
(e) F

The stage of a malignant neoplasm is a measure of the extent and degree to which it has spread. It is the most significant prognostic indicator and determines the treatment of the patient. The most frequently used staging system is that devised originally by De Noix and later adopted by the UICC, the TNM system. It should be distinguished from grading which is a microscopic evaluation of differentiation which takes into account the size and shape of neoplastic cells.

3 Epidemiology:

(a) prostate cancer is commoner in American blacks

(b) teratomas of the testicle are commoner in Jews

(c) Hawaiian Chinese are particularly at risk of colo-rectal cancer

(d) bladder cancer is commoner in petrol pump attendants

(e) gastric carcinoma is commoner in the Finnish population

4 The following are adjuncts to cancer surgery:

(a) megavoltage external beam irradiation

(b) intracavitory 198 Au colloid in malignant pleural effusion

(c) CMF chemotherapy in medullary ductal carcinoma in situ

(d) antibiotic instillation therapy

(e) interleukin 2 in renal cell carcinoma

5 The following mediate carcinogenesis:

(a) enhancer sequences that promote transcription

(b) severe endometriosis

(c) dihydrodiol epoxides

(d) sunlight

(e) the mutated P 53 gene

3 (a) T
(b) F
(c) T
(d) F
(e) T

Epidemiology is the study of disease between populations and within population groups and provide information as to the possible aetiology of the disease. Populations differ in their genetic constitution, environment, carcinogen exposure, dietary and social habits.

4 (a) T
(b) T
(c) F
(d) T
(e) T

The management of cancer requires a holistic approach with the use of a multi-disciplinary team. The team includes the surgeon, the oncologist, physiotherapists, occupational therapists, counselors and specialist nurses. Radiosensitive tumours are treated by external beam, intracavatory and unsealed radiotherapy (radio-iodine). Chemotherapy has seen its role broaden and is used as a surgical adjunct, for palliation and as neo-adjuvant therapy when it is administered prior to surgery. Antibiotic instillation therapy e.g. adriamycin is used in the treatment of superficial bladder tumours. Biological response modifiers eg TNF and interleukin 2 (activates T lymphocytes and augments endogenous host response) may also be used with benefit.

5 (a) T
(b) F
(c) T
(d) T
(e) T

A carcinogen is an agent that leads directly or indirectly to the development of a neoplasm. Carcinogens are either physical (UV light), chemical (dihydrodiol epoxides) or viral (Epstein Barr Virus) in origin and act by altering the genetic code with an increase in cellular proliferation. There follows an increase in unrepaired mistakes in DNA synthesis which become permanent mutations. If a suppressor gene such as P 53 is altered or lost the cells develop an invasive potential.

UNIT 2 CANCER SCREENING AND TREATMENT

1 The requirements of a screening programme are:

(a) an identifiable risk population

(b) no lead time bias

(c) a diagnostic test

(d) 80% compliance to screening

(e) no length bias

2 The following are aberrations of normal development and involution of the breast:

(a) fat necrosis

(b) fibrocytic disease

(c) fibroadenoma

(d) intraductal papilloma

(e) athelia

3 The following are causes of nipple discharge:

(a) bromocriptine

(b) plasma cellular mastitis

(c) puberty

(d) radiotherapy

(e) prolactinoma

1 (a) T
(b) F
(c) F
(d) F
(e) F

Screening is the presumptive identification of previously unrecognised disease. It is based on the principle that early detection leads to a better prognosis. Requirements of a screening program are a treatable condition, an identifiable target population, a sensitive and specific test, resources to apply the screening technique and to manage the detected disease and patient compliance. The test is not diagnostic but it identifies those that require further investigation.

2 (a) F
(b) T
(c) T
(d) F
(e) T

ANDI (aberration of normal development and involution) includes amastia, amazia, athelia (absence of the nipple), juvenile hypertrophy, gynaecomastia, fibroadenoma and cystic disease.

3 (a) F
(b) T
(c) F
(d) F
(e) T

Breast carcinoma may present with a sero-sanguinous discharge and therefore nipple discharge is a common cause for referral to the general surgeon. However, the commonest cause is physiological discharge (60% of women are able to expression fluid from the nipple). Other causes include periductal mastitis, duct papilloma, epithelial hyperplasia and galactorrheoa due to a prolactinoma.

4 Gynaecomastia may be caused by:

(a) liver failure

(b) cimetidine

(c) cocaine

(d) senescence

(e) aspirin

5 The following are true in breast cancer:

(a) the commonest lesion on screening is lobular carcinoma in situ

(b) positive axillary nodes occur in 4% of 1 cm cancers

(c) multifocal ductal carcinoma in situ is treated with wide local excision

(d) the Nottingham index is a prognostic indicator

(e) Madden's modified mastectomy includes division of pectoralis minor

4 (a) T
(b) T
(c) F
(d) T
(e) F

The causes of gynaecomastia are physiological (neonatal, pubertal and senile), hypogonadism, neoplasms (testicular, adrenal, pituitary), drug induced (digitalis, spironolactone, cimetidine), or due to systemic disease (liver failure, renal failure, thyrotoxicosis).

5 (a) F
(b) T
(c) F
(d) T
(e) F

The commonest lesion found in screening mammography is ductal carcinoma in-situ. When this is multifocal mastectomy is recommended. A Madden's mastectomy is a modified radical mastectomy most frequently used for cancer patients. It involves retraction but not division of pectoralis minor. Patients with lesions < 1 cm in diameter have a 4% chance of axillary node involvement and some advocate no axillary surgery. The Nottingham index is a prognostic indicator that considers the tumour grade, size and nodal involvement.

UNIT 3 TECHNIQUES OF MANAGEMENT

1 The following occur in bereavement:

(a) transposition

(b) phobias

(c) denial

(d) psychotic depression

(e) regression

2 Management of terminally ill patients include:

(a) antiemetics

(b) nasogastric feeding

(c) steroids

(d) placement of a Celestin tube

(e) PAM aid

3 In Duke's C carcinoma of the colon:

(a) 5 year survival is 25%

(b) radiotherapy reduces tumour bulk

(c) is not palliated by chemotherapy

(d) there is always transmural spread

(e) presents most commonly with blood per rectum

1 (a) T
(b) F
(c) T
(d) F
(e) F

During the initial stages of bereavement, the grief reaction may include transposition of emotions to another person. The health professionals must consider the coping strategies of anger (which may be transposed onto the staff), denial (where there is failure of acceptance of the reality), depression and anxiety. These are normal stages which may become problematic if the bereaved fails to progress along the normal bereavement pathway to resolution.

2 (a) T
(b) F
(c) T
(d) T
(e) F

The patient with a terminal illness has an established diagnosis of an incurable disease with a prognosis of at most several months. The management relies on the principle of symptom control with the treatment of pain, dysphagia, nausea, vomiting, immobility, anorexia, anaemia and bowel obstruction.

3 (a) F
(b) T
(c) F
(d) F
(e) F

Duke's C carcinoma of the colon has a 5 year survival of 35%. Radiotherapy is used to 'down stage ' the tumour and aid resection. Systemic chemotherapy may be used for the palliation of systemic spread. By definition a carcinoma of the colon is staged Duke's C when there is evidence of lymph node metastases. A change in bowel habit, weight loss and less frequently macroscopic bleeding per rectum are the commonest modes of presentation of large bowel malignancy.

4 Pain relief in terminal care may be achieved by:

(a) amitriptyline

(b) transcutaneous electrical nerve stimulation

(c) physiotherapy

(d) counselling

(e) amputation

5 Radiotherapy is indicated in the following:

(a) patients with inoperable bronchial carcinoma

(b) cosmesis or function

(c) principally in late Hodgkin's disease

(d) lower oesophageal malignancy

(e) pelvic sarcomas

4 (a) T
(b) T
(c) F
(d) T
(e) T

The management of pain in a terminally ill patient requires the attention to several factors. These include the type of analgesia (simple – paracetamol; combination – coproxamol; NSAID – ibuprofen or opiate), the routes of administration, alternatives for narcotic resistant pain (tricyclics for neuralgia; steroids for liver capsular stretch) and regional or local nerve blockade. Amputation for intractable pain may be indicated. Education by counseling establishes realistic objectives. Physiotherapy is the use of progressively graded activities such as special exercises or treatments aimed at restoring, maintaining or improving the physical (and psychological) fitness or function of an individual. Pain relief in terminally ill patients does not include physiotherapy.

5 (a) T
(b) T
(c) F
(d) F
(e) T

In cases where the operative risk is great due to coexistent disease eg recent myocardial infarction, or where the disease is advanced radiotherapy is a viable alternative to surgery patients with bronchial carcinoma. In laryngeal carcinoma radiotherapy is preferred to surgery because vocal cord function is preserved more frequently. Radiotherapy may be preferred in basal cell carcinomas close to the eye or where cosmesis dictates. Only in the early stages of Hodgkin's disease is the tumour radiosensitive. Surgery on the upper and middle third of the oesophagus carries a considerable morbidity and mortality. Radiotherapy may be used pre-operatively (neo-adjuvant) or as an alternative form of treatment in squamous cell carcinomas of the oesophagus. Tumours of the lower third are mainly radio-resistant adenocarcinomas.

UNIT 4 ETHICS AND THE LAW

1 The following are negligent in the law of tort:

(a) absence of consent

(b) failure to perform to the standard set by the law

(c) poor documentation

(d) battery

(e) unrandomised trials

2 The following statements are true regarding consent for surgery:

(a) Gillick maturity is mandatory in 14 year olds

(b) all alternative treatments must be explained

(c) unconscious patients are consented by the next of kin

(d) Jehovah's witnesses may be refused elective surgery

(e) the Mental Health Act 1983 prescribes consent for psychiatric patients

1 (a) F
(b) F
(c) F
(d) F
(e) F

Performing surgery without the informed consent of the patient is deemed to be an assault or battery. This is a criminal act and in practice rarely is cause for litigation. Most medico-legal problems arise from negligence where the plaintiff alleges that the doctor failed in his duty to treat the patient with the appropriate standard of care. In order for the litigant to be successful they must establish that the doctor had a duty of care to the patient. The standard of care (including the level of information given to the patient for consent) is that set by a responsible body of medical opinion. Poor documentation is merely an evidential problem which is particularly important where there is a long time lapse between the actual treatment and the time that legal proceedings are taken. A prospective randomised trial is the gold standard for investigation of the benefit of a new treatment. Many current treatment regimes have not passed through PRCTs.

2 (a) T
(b) T
(c) F
(d) T
(e) T

Elective surgery on children requires consent from a person competent to make informed choices on behalf of the child – usually their parents. However where the child (under 16 years of age) is deemed competent (ie able to understand the illness, proposed treatment and all its consequences) they have sufficient 'Gillick maturity'. Where the patient is unconscious the surgeon may treat them appropriately on the basis of necessity without formal informed consent. Concerning Jehovah's witnesses, undergoing elective surgery where a blood transfusion is required the surgeon may refuse to perform surgery and refer them to a colleague who is more sympathetic. Where no alternative surgeon is available eg in an emergency the surgeon may perform what is necessary to save life unless there is a pre-existing directive eg a 'living will'. Patients detained under the Mental Health Act 1983 may be treated for their psychiatric illness without consent. For non psychiatric illness attempts to perform informed consent must be made.

3 The Data Protection Act 1984 determines the following:

(a) all patients have a right of access to computerised notes

(b) confidentiality between medical staff

(c) the police may be notified of patients involved in acts of terrorism

(d) back up copies of medical notes are stored for 21 years

(e) the breach of confidentiality for notifiable disease

4 The following are requirements for consent:

(a) notification of all complications

(b) formal written consent

(c) a witness

(d) use of strict medical terminology

(e) a detailed explanation of the surgical procedure

5 Medical ethics:

(a) is guided by the Helsinki Declaration

(b) is the moral code of medical practice

(c) prohibits the use of Phase 1 drugs in humans

(d) was formalised following the First World War

(e) indicates that consent may be omitted only in war time

3 (a) T
(b) F
(c) T
(d) F
(e) F

The Data Protection Act 1984 protects patients from the misuse of their medical records and outlines the circumstances where information may be disclosed eg in the public interest (such as terrorism or serious infectious disease), risk of harm to a specific person, and to allow referral between medical specialties.

4 (a) F
(b) F
(c) F
(d) F
(e) F

Informed consent is the considered choice made by a patient who has received information concerning their illness, the proposed treatment and alternatives (including no treatment) and the consequences including the possible complications. Complications that must be mentioned are those that occur in more than 0.5% or those that may affect basic functions such as speech, reproduction etc. Written consent is not a requirement but is good supporting evidence that consent was received.

5 (a) T
(b) T
(c) T
(d) F
(e) F

After the atrocities of World War II, medical research was scrutinised and guidelines written to determine the moral code with which research would be performed. The Helsinki Declaration and the Nuremburg code embraced the ethics with which we now practice. The use of humans in Phase III trials and the requirement for informed consent were included in the draft.

UNIT 5 OUTCOME OF SURGERY

1 Requirements of surgical audit are:

(a) GMC approval

(b) confidentiality

(c) computer assisted elaboration of data

(d) three weekly meeting

(e) consultant attendance

2 Types of randomisation include:

(a) Mann-Whitney

(b) minimisation

(c) blocking

(d) stratified

(e) double blind

3 Characteristics of the ideal suture are:

(a) memory

(b) braiding

(c) half life of 10 days

(d) capillarity

(e) low friction

1 (a) F
(b) T
(c) T
(d) F
(e) T

Surgical audit is the systematic critical analysis of the quality of health care with the aim of improving its standards. For successful audit the study must be complete, continuous, consultant led, confidential, accurate, reproducible, and ideally computer aided. It is of educational value and may be used in research and as evidence in medico-legal defence. Audit is a requirement for the approval of training posts by the College of Surgeons. Regular meetings are held where juniors present audit data and discuss potential improvements.

2 (a) F
(b) T
(c) T
(d) T
(e) F

The aim of randomisation is to guarantee that the two arms of a study contain patients that are comparable in all aspects except for the treatment given. The aim is to avoid allocation bias. Types of randomisation include simple randomisation, restricted randomisation and blocking, stratified randomisation and minimisation.

3 (a) F
(b) F
(c) F
(d) F
(e) T

The ideal suture permits its use in any operation, is comfortable to handle, stimulates minimal tissue reaction, has high tensile strength in small calibre, has a low coefficient of friction, knots securely and is easy to sterilise.

4 In randomised controlled trials:

(a) type 2 error is related to sample size

(b) a steering group may advise early cessation of the trial

(c) clinical significance is when $p < 0.05$

(d) interval outcome parameters have no inherent order

(e) ethics committee approval is not required when the disease is incurable

5 Evidence based medicine:

(a) includes audit

(b) was started by Baron Larrey

(c) may involve Phase III trials

(d) does not include education

(e) has led to the cervical cancer screening programme

4 (a) T
(b) T
(c) F
(d) F
(e) F

A type I error is where the difference between the two arms of a study erroneously appear to be statistically significant. This can be avoided by lowering the p value. A type II error is the appearance of a difference between the treatment and control arm of a trial where there is in fact no difference. This error is due to the small sample size. Where the preliminary results indicate that the treatment is of significant value the steering group may call for the abortion of the trial on ethical grounds. Clinical significance is not established by statistics alone and depends on the likelihood that the results justify a change in clinical practice. Measurement of outcome may be ordinal, nominal or interval. Ordinal measurements are those where the categories have an inherent order whilst an interval measurement is characterised by a scale that reflects the same increase at all points.

5 (a) T
(b) F
(c) T
(d) F
(e) F

Evidence based medicine is the point of union between education, research and audit. Baron Larrey was the first to apply Triage in battle conditions. Cervical screening is not a result of evidence based medicine and there is little evidence of benefit, partly due to selection bias.

SYSTEM MODULE A

Locomotor System

UNIT 1 EFFECTS OF TRAUMA AND THE LOWER LIMB

1 Complications of crush injuries are:

(a) renal failure

(b) Volkmann's deformity

(c) air embolism

(d) adult respiratory distress syndrome

(e) Curling's ulcer

2 Indications for amputation include:

(a) phantom limb

(b) fixed flexion deformity

(c) metatarsalgia

(d) lipodermatosclerosis

(e) osteomyelitis

1 (a) T
(b) T
(c) F
(d) T
(e) F

Crush injuries are associated with regional ischaemia and muscle necrosis. This may be followed by the release of myoglobin and other breakdown products that block the renal tubules and cause acute tubular necrosis. An untreated increase in compartment pressure – compartment syndrome – leads to muscle fibrosis and contraction deformity. Adult respiratory distress syndrome may be caused by both thoracic crush injuries or during reperfusion of crushed regions of the body. Stress ulceration may indeed be caused by trauma, probably due to a sympathetic reflex response and catecholamine release. However Curling's ulcer refers specifically to stress ulceration following burns.

2 (a) F
(b) T
(c) T
(d) F
(e) T

Fixed flexion deformity may be debilitating and especially when associated with pain is an indication for amputation of the limb. Matatarsalgia, often found in diabetic neuropathy due to collapse of the arch in the forefoot is treated with ray amputation. Thankfully early diagnosis and antibiotic therapy has made amputation for osteomyelitis an uncommon indication for limb amputation in the developed world. Phantom limb, thought to be caused by persistence of the sensory cortex perception of the amputated limb is a complication of rather than cause of limb amputation.

3 Characteristics of osteoarthritis are:

(a) subchondral sclerosis

(b) thickened hyaline cartilage

(c) increased water content of cartilage

(d) osteophytes

(e) limited movement which is the main indication for surgery

4 The following associations are correct:

(a) Colles fracture and wrist drop

(b) suprachondylar fracture and hand ischaemia

(c) shoulder dislocation and deltoid anaesthesia

(d) posterior hip dislocation and foot drop

(e) Salmonella typhi and Pott's disease

5 In compound fractures:

(a) tetanus prophylaxis is only indicated for Gustilo and Anderson Grade > 1

(b) internal fixation is contraindicated

(c) absent arterial pulsation is treated by manipulation under Entonox

(d) elevated compartmental pressures are rare

(e) primary closure following lavage is the treatment of choice

3 (a) T
(b) F
(c) F
(d) T
(e) F

The macroscopic characteristics of osteoarthritis are thinning of hyaline cartilage, subchondral sclerosis, cysts and osteophytes. The microscopic changes are degeneration of hyaline cartilage with loss of water content. The movement of arthritic joints is limited but this does not represent an indication for surgery per se. The commonest indication for surgery is pain.

4 (a) F
(b) T
(c) T
(d) T
(e) F

Suprachondylar elbow fractures may kink or cause other injury to the brachial artery leading to ischaemia of the forearm and hand. Shoulder dislocation may injure the axillary nerve that supplies the deltoid muscle and innervates the skin over it. Posterior hip dislocation can injure the sciatic nerve. Salmonella typhi can in predisposed individuals be responsible for osteomyelitis. Pott's disease is tuberculosis of the spine.

5 (a) F
(b) F
(c) T
(d) F
(e) F

Tetanus prophylaxis is indicated in all compound fractures unless the patient is already immunised. Internal fixation is possible in all but the most dirty compound fractures. The absence of distal pulses (in the presence of contralateral pulses) in a fractured limb requires immediate attention. Manipulation of the limb under Entonox to restore the normal pulsation is indicated. Only in cases where the wound associated with the fracture is absolutely uncontaminated should primary closure be contemplated.

UNIT 2 INFECTIONS AND THE UPPER LIMB

1 The following statements concerning gas gangrene are true:

(a) the haemolysin of Clostridium perfringens destroys fat

(b) low oxygen tension inhibits bacterial growth

(c) may be seen on X-ray

(d) leads to Fournier's gangrene

(e) is characterised by crepitus

2 In acute pyogenic osteomyelitis:

(a) life threatening septicaemia is a presentation in neonates

(b) organisms settle near the metaphysis at the growing end of a long bone

(c) plain X-rays show no abnormality for 3 weeks

(d) the sequestrum appears radioluscent compared to surrounding bone

(e) S aureus is the commonest infecting agent

1 (a) T
(b) F
(c) T
(d) F
(e) T

Gas gangrene is relevant to military, trauma and colorectal surgery. Clostridium perfringens, a spore bearing obligate anaerobic bacillus, releases collagenase, hyaluronidase, haemolysin and other proteases. The wound infections are extremely painful and characterised by crepitus. Gas within the tissues may be noticed on plain radiographs. Synergistic spreading gangrene – necrotising fascitis – is not caused by clostridia but a mixture of other aerobic and anaerobic organisms.

2 (a) T
(b) T
(c) F
(d) F
(e) T

Acute osteomyelitis caused in 80% of cases by Staphylococcus aureus was often a fatal condition in children due to the septicaemia associated with it. The disease nearly always begins at the metaphysis, a particularly well perfused part of growing bone. The disease then progresses through the cortex via the Haversian canals causing thrombosis of the blood vessels within the bone. There are no abnormal radiological findings for up to 10 days, the first features being new bone deposition by the elevated periosteum. Later an island of necrotic bone – the sequestrum – appears as a radiodense area within a rarefied area of bone.

3 The following associations are true concerning Brachial plexus injuries:

(a) Erb-Duchenne and C5 C6 roots

(b) poor prognosis and Horner's syndrome

(c) Klumpke and clawed hand

(d) breech delivery and thenar wasting

(e) complete root avulsion and cervical meningocoele

4 Carpal tunnel syndrome:

(a) is caused by acromegaly

(b) is common following Colles fracture

(c) is associated with paresis of abductor pollicis longus in 25%

(d) 10% have little or no improvement following surgery

(e) is treated with diuretics

5 The following are stable fractures of the spine:

(a) fracture in a fused spine (eg ankylosing spondylitis)

(b) transverse process fractures

(c) burst fractures

(d) fracture of the atlas

(e) compression fractures

3 (a) T
(b) T
(c) T
(d) F
(e) T

Upper brachial plexus lesions – Erb-Duchenne – affects the 5th and sometimes 6th cervical nerve roots affecting the biceps, brachialis, brachioradialis, supinator brevis, spinati and deltoid muscles. It may be associated with a breech delivery but does not affect the small muscles of the hand. Avulsion injuries carry a worse prognosis the more proximal the damage. Horner's syndrome implies injury to T 1 root and will therefore carry a poor prognosis.

4 (a) T
(b) F
(c) F
(d) T
(e) T

Carpal tunnel syndrome may be caused by compression of the tunnel walls (eg acromegaly, rarely Colles fracture), compression within the tunnel or changes in the median nerve. Abductor pollicis brevis is affected. The first line of therapy for mild symptoms include splintage, corticosteroids, diuretics and rest. A recognised complication of surgical treatment (offered to those with severe or persistent symptoms) is that up to 10% of patients show no improvement.

5 (a) T
(b) F
(c) T
(d) F
(e) T

To establish the stability of a spine fracture one should consider the three columns: anterior (vertebral bodies, intervertebral discs and longitudinal ligaments), intermediate (facetal joints and ligaments), and posterior (spinous processes and interspinous ligaments). A fracture involving one column alone is stable. Fractures involving more than one column will tend to be unstable, with maximum instability when all three columns are affected.

UNIT 3 BONE DISEASE AND SPINE

1 Congenital Talipes Equinovarus:

(a) is caused by failure of growth of tibialis posterior

(b) the muscles function abnormally

(c) the foot is pulled upwards

(d) cure is achieved by early treatment

(e) is treated in adult life with a triple arthrodiesis

2 Paget's disease of the bone:

(a) leads to Paget's sarcoma

(b) is confirmed on isotopic bone scan by increased uptake

(c) will show sclerosis and osteoporosis on X-ray

(d) is treated symptomatically with Calcium

(e) increases the incidence of osteoarthritis

1 (a) T
(b) F
(c) F
(d) F
(e) T

Congenital Talipes Equinovarus – club foot – affects 1 to 2 per 1,000 live births. The talus points downwards and slightly outwards while the entire forefoot is shifted medially and rotated into supination. There is a reduced growth of tibialis posterior but the muscle is not abnormal in function. The treatment of this difficult condition is controversial and there are differing opinions on the timing and nature of surgery. However cure is not achieved. At an early stage posterior, medial and plantar soft tissue release are likely to be required. In the adult a triple arthrodesis may be performed.

2 (a) T
(b) T
(c) T
(d) F
(e) T

Paget's disease or osteitis deformans is a disease of unknown aetiology of increasing incidence. Its incidence increases with age with it affecting 10% of men over 90 years of age. The primary event appears to be an abnormal increase in the activity and proliferation of osteoclasts. There follows an excessive and haphazard bone resorbtion followed by a compensatory increase in osteoblastic activity giving the alternation of osteoporosis and sclerosis seen on X-ray. A bone scan shows markedly increased uptake in the involved areas of the skeleton. Many patients are asymptomatic and require no treatment. Others may require simple analgesics. Calcitonin and biphosphonates may be given to reduce bone resorbtion. There is no role for calcium supplementation, indeed the calcium and phosphate levels are normal. The complications of Paget's disease are pathological fractures, osteoarthritis (may develop in joints adjacent to diseased bone but does not necessarily increase the overall incidence compared to a similarly aged population), spinal stenosis, deafness and osteosarcoma which has an increased incidence in patients with Paget's disease.

3 The following statements regarding neural injury are true:

(a) flaccid paralysis and visceral paralysis occur below the cord lesion

(b) traumatic paraplegia may be successfully treated with laminectomy

(c) injury at the 1st lumbar vertebra produces cord and nerve root injury

(d) persistence of perianal sensation suggests an incomplete lesion

(e) the spine is fixed immediately to facilitate nursing care

4 The following are causes of low back pain:

(a) osteoid osteoma

(b) defect of neural arch

(c) Fanconi's anaemia

(d) von Recklinghausen's disease

(e) Erhlers Danlos syndrome

5 Congenital dysplasia of the hip:

(a) is common in Northern Italy

(b) results in abduction of less than 70 degrees

(c) is bilateral in 50% of cases

(d) shows a small capital nucleus on the affected side

(e) when bilateral leads to narrowing of the perineal gap

3 (a) T
(b) F
(c) T
(d) T
(e) T

Following spinal injury, spinal shock with abolition of voluntary power, sensation and reflex activity occurs. Subsequently flaccid paralysis will remain distal to the site of complete injury. The spinal cord ends at L1/2 so injury at L1 will involve the cord and nerve roots. Absence of perianal sensation following the resolution of spinal shock is a poor prognostic sign. The cardinal rule in the assessment and management of a patient with suspected spinal injury is that the vertebral injury is unstable until proven otherwise. Hence fixation is essential to prevent further injury and to facilitate nursing.

4 (a) T
(b) T
(c) F
(d) T
(e) F

Lower back pain is common. The causes of the pain are not always so.

5 (a) T
(b) T
(c) F
(d) T
(e) F

The incidence of hip dysplasia is 2 per 1,000 births. In Europe it is commoner in northern Italy, France and Wales. It is five times commoner in girls than boys and is bilateral in 25% of cases. The nucleus of ossification in the head of the femur of the affected side is smaller than the normal side. The perineal gap is widened in patients with bilateral disease.

SYSTEM MODULE B

Vascular

UNIT 1 ARTERIAL DISEASES

1 The following statements regarding peripheral vascular disease are true:

(a) mild claudication is associated with an ankle brachial index of 0.6

(b) in diabetics distal ischaemia may exist in the presence of strong dorsalis pedis and posterior tibial pulses

(c) the six Ps are specific to acute embolisation

(d) profunda femoris is the most commonly diseased vessel in the leg

(e) in trash foot the distal pulses are not present

2 Amputations:

(a) below knee amputation should be less than 15 cm from the tibial tuberosity

(b) ray amputation is performed in diabetics

(c) above knee amputations are placed > 20 cm from the greater trochanter

(d) is complicated by causalgia

(e) Gritti-Stokes amputation is popular with the prosthetist because of its long stump

1 (a) T
(b) T
(c) F
(d) F
(e) F

Segmental Doppler limb pressure is a widely accepted non invasive technique in the assessment of peripheral vascular disease. A normal ankle brachial index is 0.9–1. The claudication range is 0.6–0.8. Values less than 0.5 may be associated with rest pain. Doppler readings are unreliable in diabetics due to vessel incompressibility. The six Ps refer to acute arterial insufficiency of any cause. The superficial femoral artery is the most commonly affected vessel, the profunda vessel is usually spared. A trash foot results from showers of emboli (eg from a popliteal aneurysm) that occlude distal vessels, this may occur in the presence of ankle pulses

2 (a) F
(b) T
(c) T
(d) T
(e) F

80% of ischaemic gangrene leads to a below knee amputation. In a long posterior flap, the skin incision should be 15 cm below the tibial tuberosity anteriorly and at the level of the achilles tendon origin posteriorly. The ray amputation is performed in diabetics to treat the collapse of the forefoot arch due to peripheral neuropathy. The complications of amputation are haematoma formation, infection, ischaemic necrosis, osteomyelitis, spurs and osteophytes, ulceration, stump neuroma, phantom limb, causalgia, jactitation, aneurysm, AV fistula, flexion deformity, muscle herniation and non union. The Gritti-Stokes amputation has a longer stump compared to the above knee amputation but it is not possible to fit an internal knee mechanism in the prosthesis.

3 The following statements regarding aortic aneurysms are true:

(a) the male to female ratio is 5 to 1 or more

(b) 2% are suprarenal

(c) risk of rupture is not related to the diameter

(d) increase in size is related to cotinine levels

(e) overall mortality following rupture is > 70%

4 Investigations in vascular surgery:

(a) carotid doppler directly measures vessel stenosis

(b) obesity increases complications of angiography

(c) angiography is contraindicated in the presence of sepsis

(d) two views are required in pelvic and carotid angiography

(e) MRI angiography enables visualisation up to the Circle of Willis in investigation of carotid disease

5 Surgical treatment of cerebrovascular disease:

(a) A transient ischaemic attack is a neurological dysfunction with complete resolution within 48 hours

(b) A reversible ischaemic neurological deficit involves complete resolution of signs within 2 weeks

(c) Asymptomatic carotid stenosis > 75% require surgery

(d) Stroke in evolution is a contraindication to surgery

(e) Recurrent laryngeal nerve injury is a complication of carotid endarterectomy

3 (a) T
(b) F
(c) F
(d) T
(e) T

5% of abdominal aortic aneurysms are suprarenal. The risk of rupture is directly related to the diameter of the aneurysm. This is estimated at 4% per annum for a 5 cm aortic aneurysm, 9% for a 6 cm aneurysm and 19% for a 7 cm aneurysm. Cotinine is a metabolite of nicotine and is related to increasing size of the aneurysm. 50% of ruptured abdominal aortic aneurysms do not reach hospita. There is a 50% mortality for patients who reach hospital alive.

4 (a) F
(b) T
(c) T
(d) T
(e) T

Carotid Doppler measures blood flow. At the site of stenosis doppler measures the increased blood flow through the narrowing. Obesity increases the difficulty of vascular access and the presence of skin sepsis including inter-trigo increases the risk of introducing infection. Two views are required in pelvic and carotid angiography to ascertain accurately the degree of stenosis. Magnetic Resonance Angiography is a new method of visualisation of the Circle of Willis following sub-arachnoid haemorrhage.

5 (a) F
(b) T
(c) F
(d) F
(e) T

A transient ischaemic attack implies resolution of symptoms within 24 hours of the clinical presentation. If symptoms have not completely resolved up to but not beyond 2 weeks this is termed a RIND. Asymptomatic carotid artery stenosis is currently the subject of a randomised controlled trial to establish the value of carotid endarterectomy in this group; the jury is out. Strokes in evolution may undergo carotid endarterectomy in some specialist centres.

UNIT 2 VENOUS DISEASES

1 The following statements regarding venous ulcers are true:

(a) varicosities are the common denominator in the pathophysiology of venous ulcers

(b) venous ulcers are commoner in multiple sclerosis patients

(c) four layer compression bandaging may give compression of up to 40 mmHg

(d) varicose ulcers occur on the anterior or lateral ankle surface

(e) compression bandaging is contraindicated in ankle-brachial pressure indexes < 0.8

2 Deep venous thrombosis:

(a) 50% of all deep venous thromboses occur in the legs and pelvis

(b) the incidence of DVT in patients undergoing hip surgery is 60% if no prophylactic measures are taken

(c) damage to the endothelial lining contributes to Virchow's triad

(d) 98% of all pulmonary emboli arise from thromboses in the leg and pelvis

(e) patients with recurrent venous thrombosis are screened for occult malignancy

1 (a) F
(b) T
(c) T
(d) T
(e) F

Venous ulcers occur where there is venous insufficiency or following deep venous thrombosis in which the valves have been destroyed following recanalisation. In both, the common denominator is venous stasis. The use of compression bandaging or a strong graduated compression stocking exerts 40 mmHg at the ankle. ABPI of 0.6 is a contraindication for compression bandaging.

2 (a) F
(b) T
(c) T
(d) T
(e) T

The pelvis and calf are the most common sites for DVT. The risk factors for DVT are hip and pelvic surgery, surgery of malignancy, prolonged operations, immobility, and age. Damage to the endothelium, stasis of blood and increased coagulability are predisposing factors that lead to venous thrombosis and is called Virchow's triad. Thrombophlebitis migrans may indicate the presence of visceral cancer eg pancreatic

3 Varicose veins:

(a) permit blood flow in both directions

(b) inheritance has been established

(c) non symptomatic varicosities warrant surgery

(d) tributary recurrence after saphenous surgery is treated with injection sclerotherapy

(e) require investigation with ascending phlebograms

4 Axillary and subclavian vein thrombosis:

(a) account for 2% of all venous thromboses

(b) affects the right hand more than the left

(c) is also known as Effort's thrombosis

(d) treatment is required in patients who present late

(e) most untreated patients are symptom free at 2 weeks

5 Investigations in venous disease:

(a) Venous doppler reliably identifies proximal venous obstruction only

(b) Isotopic iodine fibrinogen scanning is the most sensitive and specific test for venous thrombosis

(c) Decreased compressibility of the vein wall is a diagnostic feature of thrombosis on duplex scanning

(d) Plethysmography studies the change in volume of a limb

(e) A positive Homan's sign indicates the need for venous thrombectomy

3 (a) T
(b) T
(c) F
(d) T
(e) F

A varicose vein is a dilated, elongated and tortuous vein. Sapheno-femoral valve incompetence can be familial. The indications for surgery are bleeding, discomfort, cosmesis and venous ulceration. The investigation of choice for varicose veins is colour flow doppler.

4 (a) T
(b) T
(c) T
(d) F
(e) F

The increase in incidence of axillary and subclavian vein thrombosis is related to the use of the latter for central venous access. Effort thrombosis occurs usually in the dominant arm after use and represents venous thrombosis. Treatment with heparinisation and warfarinisation is most effective when the diagnosis is made early. The organised thrombus is less responsive to anticoagulant treatment.

5 (a) T
(b) F
(c) T
(d) T
(e) F

Venous Doppler is a cheap non invasive investigation for the investigation of proximal venous obstruction. Below the knee the sensitivity is reduced. Despite the specificity of the fibrinogen scan it is unreliable in proximal venous thrombi and is not recommended as a single test for venous thrombosis. Veins which under normal circumstances are compressible lose this feature when thrombosed.

UNIT 3 LYMPHATICS AND SPLEEN

1 Lymphoedema:

(a) affects the leg in 80% of cases
(b) is most commonly iatrogenic in aetiology
(c) presents with unilateral limb swelling
(d) delays transport of Rhenium-Antimony complexes in the peripheral lymph
(e) is treated by Homan's procedure which is lymphatic by-pass operation

2 Indications for splenectomy include:

(a) beta thalassaemia major
(b) myelofibrosis
(c) Banti's syndrome
(d) Von Willebrand's disease
(e) pyrexia of unknown origin

1 (a) T
(b) F
(c) T
(d) T
(e) F

Lymphoedema is the accumulation of tissue fluid as a result of a fault in the lymphatic system. It most commonly effects the legs, arm, genitalia and face. Primary lymphoedema is of unknown cause whilst secondary lymphoedema is due to radiotherapy surgery or infection (filariasis). Lyphoedema must be distinguished from systemic disease (cardiac or renal failure), venous disease (post-thrombotic syndrome) or rarer causes of limb enlargement (arterio-venous malformation). Delayed ilio-inguinal uptake of radio-nucleotide Rhenium-Antimony labelled technetium is diagnostic. Treatments include debulking operations (Homan's procedure), lymphovenous shunts and lymphatic bypass.

2 (a) T
(b) T
(c) T
(d) F
(e) T

The indications for splenectomy are following rupture, primary hypersplenism (beta thalassaemia major, hereditary spherocytosis), secondary hypersplenism (myelofibrosis, Banti's syndrome), splenic tumours, diagnosis (PUO) and staging Hodgkin's disease (replaced by radiological investigations).

3 The following statements concerning systemic sclerosis are true:

(a) skin changes and puffiness are late features

(b) macrostomia is due to fibrosis

(c) dysphagia is due to oesophageal hypomotility

(d) patients may succumb to pseudo-cardiomyopathy

(e) anti-centromere bodies are characteristic of the Crest syndrome

4 Cervical lymphadenopathy:

(a) is the second commonest cause of a swelling in the neck

(b) is caused by toxoplasmosis

(c) leads to a collar stud abscess in syphilis

(d) of the upper node occurs in submandibular gland carcinomas

(e) occurs in Reticulosarcoma

5 Treatment of Haemophilia includes:

(a) stored whole plasma

(b) fresh plasma

(c) fresh serum within 10 hours

(d) cryoprecipitate

(e) gamma-globulins

3 (a) F
(b) F
(c) F
(d) T
(e) T

Systemic sclerosis may present early with non-pitting oedema of the skin and later with a tight, waxy, and then atrophic skin with increased pigmentation. Though the skin is most commonly affected, the lungs, muscles, heart, kidney and gastrointestinal system are also affected. Dysphagia is caused by sclerosis of the collagen in the oesophagus and when part of the CREST syndrome (Calcinosis cutis, Raynaud's phenomenon, oesophageal immotility, sclerodactyly and telangectasia) due to oesophageal hypomotility.

4 (a) F
(b) T
(c) F
(d) F
(e) T

The commonest cause of a neck swelling is an enlarged lymph gland which in turn is most commonly due to infection (non-specific, tuberculosis, glandular fever and toxoplasmosis) or tumour deposits. The 'pointing' of caseous material through the deep cervical fascia into subcutaneous tissues is called a collar stud abscess and is characteristic of Tb. Malignancy of the submandibular gland metastasise to the middle deep cervical lymph nodes. Primary reticuloses such as lymphomas and some sarcomas may also cause cervical lymphadenopathy.

5 (a) F
(b) T
(c) F
(d) T
(e) F

Haemophilia A is due to factor VIII deficiency and Haemophilia B (Christmas disease) due to factor IX deficiency. Treatment consists of purified factor VIII or IX. The cryoprecipitate or fresh frozen plasma may be used.

SYSTEM MODULE C

Head, neck, endocrine and paediatric

UNIT 1 THE HEAD

1 Quinsy:

(a) is a peritonsillar abscess

(b) presence with excessive salivation and muffled speech

(c) the abscess points into the floor of the mouth

(d) inflammation of the lateral pterygoid muscle limits mouth opening

(e) a lateral X-ray of the neck is diagnostic

2 Penetrating injuries to the eye:

(a) should be suspected in the presence of an irregular pupil

(b) demand urgent surgical repair

(c) Acetazolamide should be avoided in these cases

(d) result in loss of eye sight

(e) siderosis follows retention of ferrous foreign bodies

1 (a) T
(b) T
(c) F
(d) F
(e) T

Quinsy is a peritonsillar abscess. It occurs when tonsillitis extends to involve the tonsillar bed. It presents with excess salivation and trismus which impairs speech. The abscess tends to point in the soft palate that represents the route of least resistance and if the medial pterigoid is involved mouth opening is impaired. A lateral X-ray of the neck will confirm the presence and define the extent of the abscess.

2 (a) T
(b) T
(c) F
(d) F
(e) T

An irregular pupil and prolapse of intraocular eye contents warrants careful examination under anaesthesia for a penetrating eye injury. The integrity of the globe must be corrected immediately. Acetazolamide lowers the intraocular pressure. Immediate surgery by an experienced eye surgeon considerably improves the prognosis and thus these injuries rarely lead to loss of sight. Metallic foreign bodies are identified by X-ray. Non-metallic foreign bodies may be visualised by ultrasound.

3 Hydrocephalus:

(a) presents in infancy with abducent nerve palsy

(b) in older children is accompanied by obesity and reduced skeletal growth

(c) is caused by sub-arachnoid haemorrhage

(d) is called Hydrocephalus ex vacuo when associated with dementia

(e) in adults is characterised by transient rises in intracranial pressure

4 Epistaxis:

(a) may be caused by arterial or venous bleeding

(b) is most commonly caused by epistaxis digitorum

(c) in 90% of cases comes from the antero-superior portion of the septum (Little's area)

(d) is treated by blowing the nose to remove clots and pinching the nose for 10 minutes

(e) of posterior origin is treated by insertion of a Foley catheter

5 Pleiomorphic adenoma of the salivary gland:

(a) appears most commonly in the elderly

(b) is commoner in females

(c) is cystic in nature

(d) is not tender to palpation

(e) is bilateral in 10% of patients

3 (a) T
(b) T
(c) T
(d) F
(e) T

Hydrocephalus is the imbalance between the ratio of the CSF to cerebral tissue within the cranium. The presenting signs depend upon the age of the patient at presentation. In the neonatal period an increase of the skull circumference, distended tense fontanelles and failure to thrive may be the only clues. In more marked cases an abducens palsy and 'sunsetting eyes' may be present. Hydrocephalus may follow subarachnoid haemorrhage by interfering with the passive process of CSF reabsorbtion at the arachnoid villi. The ex-vacuo variety of hydrocephalus is due to the shrinking of the brain with age, a phenomenon that may occur without any deterioration in mental faculties.

4 (a) T
(b) T
(c) F
(d) T
(e) T

Epistaxis may be arterial or venous in origin. In 90% of cases it originates from Little's area, a plexus of veins on the antero-inferior portion of the septum. The commonest cause is epistaxis digitorum, also known as nose picking. The treatment involves sitting the patient so as to avoid blood running posteriorly into the throat, blowing the nose then pinching the nostrils to tamponade the bleeding. In posterior bleeds a Foley catheter may be used with good effect.

5 (a) F
(b) F
(c) F
(d) T
(e) F

Pleomorphic adenomas are slow growing lesions that occur equally in men and women and have a peak incidence in the 5th decade. It presents as a slow growing solid mass that is usually not tender to palpation. Pleomorphic adenomas are rarely bilateral unlike Warthin's tumour.

UNIT 2 NECK AND ENDOCRINE GLANDS

1 The following are associated with hyperparathyroidism:

(a) raised serum calcium

(b) peptic ulcer

(c) cataract

(d) paravertebral ossification

(e) aortic stenosis

2 The following statements regarding neck swellings are true:

(a) a pharyngeal pouch appears behind the sternomastoid muscle

(b) torticollis is associated with a 'sternomastoid tumour'

(c) a branchial sinus or fistula is the remnant of the third branchial cleft

(d) a chemodectoma is found at the level of the hyoid cartilage

(e) cystic hygromas do not transilluminate due to a dusky content

1 (a) T
(b) T
(c) T
(d) F
(e) F

Parathyroid hormone increases serum calcium levels at the expense of phosphate. In 70% of cases the condition is asymptomatic. Symptomatic forms are traditionally described as 'stones' (nephrolithiasis and nephrocalcinosis), 'bones' (bone pains and arthralgia), 'groans' (peptic ulcer disease and pancreatitis – both caused by hypercalcaemia) and 'psychic overtones'. Calcium may increase the secretion of gastrin which in turn may lead to peptic ulceration. The calcium may deposit in the eye leading to cataract formation.

2 (a) T
(b) T
(c) F
(d) T
(e) F

Neck swellings are an exam favourite. For diagnosis of neck swellings, the examination should identify the site (anterior or posterior triangle) and differentiate single from multiple swellings and solid from cystic swellings. Multiple lumps tend to be lymph nodes. Single lumps in the anterior triangle that move on swallowing are either thyroid swellings or a thyroglossal cyst. Lumps in the anterior triangle that do not move on swallowing include lymph nodes, carotid body tumours, cold abscesses and branchial cysts. Lumps in the posterior triangle include lymph nodes, cystic hygromas, pharyngeal triangle include lymph ndes, cystic hygromos, pharyngeal pouches and subclavian aneurysms.

3 The following statements regarding the thyroid gland are true:

(a) TSH causes thyroid enlargement

(b) only the thyroid gland can concentrate Iodide

(c) thyroxine is carried mainly bound to protein in the plasma

(d) Iodide blocks the release of thyroxine

(e) mono-iodothyronin is released in the serum

4 The following are surgically treatable causes of systemic hypertension:

(a) Cushing's disease

(b) fibromuscular hyperplasia of the renal arteries

(c) Conn's syndrome

(d) atrial myxomas

(e) tumours of the Organ of Zuckerlandl

5 Complications of thyroid surgery include:

(a) carpal spasm

(b) altered intonation

(c) air embolism

(d) psychosis

(e) airway compression

3 (a) T
(b) F
(c) T
(d) T
(e) F

In non-toxic goitres the enlargement of the thyroid gland is due to increased secretion of TSH due to diminished production of thyroid hormones. T4 and T3 are bound to the specific thyroxine-binding globulin (TBG) and to a lesser degree albumin in the blood. Mono-iodothyronin is coupled to di-iodothyronin to form tri-iododothyronin in the follicular cells of the thyroid gland.

4 (a) T
(b) T
(c) T
(d) F
(e) T

The characteristic feature of adrenal tumours and hyperplasias is that they are small and may be the cause of hypertension. Cushing's disease with excess corticosteroids that have a mineralocorticoid effect; Conn's syndrome with excess aldosterone; phaeochromocytomas with catecholamine release. Fibromuscular hyperplasia of the renal arteries responds well – better than atherosclerosis – to angioplasty.

5 (a) T
(b) T
(c) T
(d) F
(e) T

Hypoparathyroidism may complicate total thyroidectomies if the parathyroids are inadvertently removed or devascularised. Hypocalcaemia may follow and present with carpal or pedal spasm. Injury to the external/superior laryngeal nerves may affect the tone of the voice. Air embolism may occur following the opening of large veins in the neck. Airway compromise may be due to bilateral vocal cord paresis or compression secondary to a haematoma in the pre-tracheal space.

UNIT 3 PAEDIATRIC DISORDERS

1 Hypertrophic pyloric stenosis in infants:

(a) occurs in 3 in every 1,000 births

(b) in 7% of cases is familial

(c) characteristically effects first born female infants

(d) bile is present in late stages of vomiting

(e) blood is present in the stool

2 Cleft lip and palate:

(a) the incidence is decreasing

(b) is familial

(c) repair of the cleft lip is best performed at six months

(d) the most popular repair is the Millard

(e) the risk of middle ear infections is increased

3 Neonatal surgery:

(a) incubators are used principally to prevent trauma

(b) the operating theatre is kept at a higher temperature

(c) infants with intestinal obstruction all require nasogastric intubation

(d) overhydration is compensated by diuresis in the first week of life

(e) transverse abdominal incisions are preferred

1 (a) T
(b) T
(c) F
(d) F
(e) F

Hypertrophic pyloric stenosis is caused by the thickening of the circular muscle layer of the pylorus. It occurs in 3 in every 1,000 births with a 4:1 male predominance. Approximately 7% or more have a familiarity for the disorder. Sons of affected mothers have a 20% risk of being affected. Bile is not present in the vomitus though blood may be if oesophagitis follows.

2 (a) F
(b) T
(c) F
(d) T
(e) T

Cleft lip results from abnormal development of the medial nasal and maxillary processes. Cleft palate results from the failure of fusion of the two palatine processes. The incidence is about 1.25/1,000 live births in the U.K and appears to be stable or increasing depending on the region of the world. The repair of the lip – the Millard repair – is usually done at 8–12 weeks but can be performed in the neonatal period to reduce middle ear drainage problems in the future and help parental bonding.

3 (a) F
(b) T
(c) T
(d) F
(e) T

Neonatal emergency surgery is required in 100 in every 25,000 births. These patients are best managed in specialist units. Paediatric and neonatal physiology requires close temperature, respiratory, renal and nutritional care. The role of the incubator is to provide the appropriate (higher) ambient temperature for the child. The risk of aspiration pneumonia in neonates is higher than in adults and is avoided by the insertion of a paediatric nasogastric tube. Renal immaturity renders intrinsic fluid balance precarious, fluid balance must therefore be judicious. The shape of the abdomen makes access better with transverse incisions. They are also less painful and heal better.

4 Hirschsprung's disease:

(a) affects 1 in 2,000 children

(b) has an increased incidence in Down's syndrome

(c) aganglionosis is present in the grossly dilated bowel

(d) diagnosis is indicated by an excess of positively staining nerve trunks

(e) definitive surgery is by Soave or Duhamel operation

5 Intussusception:

(a) is commoner in girls than boys

(b) has its highest incidence in the first month of life

(c) in 45% of cases an identifiable anatomical lead point is present

(d) redcurrant jelly stool is passed after the first 24 hours of onset

(e) surgery is indicated following failure of hydrostatic reduction

4 (a) F
(b) T
(c) F
(d) T
(e) T

Hirschsprung's disease is the commonest cause of neonatal intestinal obstruction with an incidence of 1 in 5,000. It appears to be more common in boys and in up to 10% of cases is associated with Down's syndrome. The neurological mural defect lays in the bowel immediately distal to the dilated colon due to its inability to expand. The diagnosis is made by a rectal biopsy which reveals the absence of ganglion cells and an excess of positively staining nerve trunks on histological staining for cholinesterase. Initial surgical management involves placement of a defunctioning colostomy. The definitive operation is performed at 6 months or more and consists of a resection of the diseased segment and anastomosis as described by Soave, Duhamel and Swenson.

5 (a) F
(b) F
(c) F
(d) T
(e) T

Intussusception is the invagination of one portion of the intestine into the lumen of an adjacent segment of bowel. The incidence is 4–5 per 1,000 children and it is commoner in boys. It is rare in the first month of life but overall is commonest in the first year. The lead point that invaginates (a polyp, Meckel's, lymphomas etc) is only identifiable in 10% of cases and should be resected. The clinical features are of an intestinal colic. The so called redcurrent jelly stool is a late feature occurring 24 hours after the onset of symptoms. The first line of treatment after resuscitation is hydrostatic reduction with the use of an enema. Failure or repeated recurrence is an indication for surgery.

System Module D

Abdomen

Unit 1 Abdominal wall

1 The following statements regarding irreducible hernia are true:

(a) an incarcerated hernia has no obstruction or interference with the blood supply

(b) strangulated hernias have compromised blood supply

(c) irreducible hernias are best managed by manipulation and reduction

(d) obstructed herniae are the commonest cause of small bowel obstruction in elderly

(e) adhesions develop between the sac and its contents in incarcerated herniae

2 The following predispose to development of herniae:

(a) ascites

(b) benign prostatic hypertrophy

(c) nerve damage

(d) tendency to keloid scar formation

(e) immobilisation

1 (a) T
(b) T
(c) F
(d) T
(e) T

Herniae are incarcerated (irreducible), strangulated or obstructed. An incarcerated hernia need not be obstructed or strangulated. Manipulation and reduction (taxis) is not recommended since the neck of the hernia often develops a fibrous constricting band which returns with the hernia into the abdominal cavity and may give rise to obstruction.

2 (a) T
(b) T
(c) T
(d) F
(e) F

Causes of raised intra-abdominal pressures increase the likelihood of herniae developing. The division of the ilioinguinal nerve following appendicectomy is proposed to increase the incidence of right sided inguinal herniae.

3 Concerning the anatomy of herniae:

(a) direct herniae are a result of a weak transversalis fascia

(b) a femoral hernia presents with a lump below and medial to the pubic tubercle

(c) the antimesenteric border of the bowel is trapped in a Richter's hernia

(d) Littre's hernia contains a Meckel's diverticulum

(e) an obtruator hernia lies deep to pectineus

4 Discharge from the umbilicus may be due to the following:

(a) falciform ligament

(b) abscess in a urachal cyst

(c) patent urachus

(d) mammary duct fistula

(e) endometriosis

5 The following statements concerning access to the abdomen are true:

(a) muscle splitting incisions are more painful than cutting incisions

(b) failure to close the peritoneum increases the incidenc of adhesions

(c) collagenase diisolves the suture near wound edges

(d) the Veress needle in laparoscopic procedures is inserted under direct vision

(e) burst abdomen is preceded by a sero-sanguinous discharge

3 (a) T
(b) F
(c) T
(d) T
(e) T

The neck of a femoral hernia presents below and lateral to the pubic tubercle in contrast to the inguinal hernia which presents above and medial to the pubic tubercle. In a Richter's hernia the sac contains only a portion of the bowel wall. Rare external herniae are the interparietal hernia (Spigelian), herniae of the triangle of Petit (Lumbar), and perineal herniae.

4 (a) F
(b) T
(c) T
(d) F
(e) T

The umbilicus may discharge where there is inflammation (omphalitits, endometriosis, dermatitis or a granuloma), neoplasm, fistulae (patent urachus or a patent vitello-intestinal duct) or a calculus.

5 (a) F
(b) F
(c) F
(d) F
(e) T

Cutting through muscle produces more post-operative pain than muscle splitting incisions where the anatomical planes between muscle fibres are used. There is no evidence that closing the peritoneum reduces the development of adhesions. The release of collagenase near wound edges weakens the skin and therefore sutures should be placed 1 cm away. The tip of the first trocar cannot be visualised before the camera is inserted unless a small laparotomy incision is made. The 'pink sign' indicates impending wound disruption.

UNIT 2 ACUTE ABDOMINAL CONDITIONS

1 The following factors favour diffusion of peritonitis:

(a) peristalsis

(b) corticosteroids

(c) infancy

(d) bed rest

(e) obesity

2 In fulminating ulcerative colitis:

(a) the temperature by definition exceeds 40°C

(b) low High Density lipoprotein signifies a severe attack

(c) plain abdominal films confirm toxic megacolon

(d) the diarrhoea contains predominately blood with minimal mucus

(e) barium enema is useful to identify those patients requiring surgery

3 Following abdominal trauma the following are required as part of the secondary survey:

(a) eviscerated bowel is returned to the abdomen in a warm sterile pack

(b) diagnostic peritoneal lavage is indicated where assessment is difficult

(c) the back is examined for ecchymosis

(d) auscultation is performed to exclude bowel injury

(e) ultrasound scanning is used to identify the presence of free fluid

1 (a) T
(b) T
(c) T
(d) F
(e) F

Peritonitis is usually bacterial. The most important factor favouring the diffusion of peritonitis is the rate at which the peritonitis develops. Protective mechanisms to protect the peritoneal cavity from spread are absent in the early stages.

2 (a) F
(b) F
(c) T
(d) T
(e) F

Fulminating UC has a temperature between 38.9 and 39.4°C. Low serum albumin is associated with a severe attack and a toxic dilatation of the colon may occur. The diarrhoea contains blood, pus and mucus. The indication for surgery is determined primarily by clinical assessment and the basic investigations including a plain abdominal X-ray.

3 (a) F
(b) T
(c) T
(d) F
(e) F

The secondary survey is a top to toe assessment of the patient whilst continuing resuscitation and review. The auscultation of bowel sounds is unreliable following trauma. Diagnostic peritoneal lavage is useful where patients are difficult to assess and a laparotomy is considered. Though ultrasound is useful, urgent treatment should not be delayed for investigations and therefore ultrasound is not considered part of the secondary survey.

4 The following statements concerning acute intestinal obstruction are true:

(a) strangulation is less dangerous in external herniae compared to intraperitoneal herniae

(b) stercoral ulceration occurs in closed loop obstruction

(c) attacks of intestinal colic last for 1 to 2 minutes

(d) right iliac fossa tenderness indicates imminent caecal perforation

(e) following prolonged vomiting the vomitus contains faeces

5 In fulminant pancreatitis:

(a) fat necroses of the omentum is found

(b) hypercalcaemia is a marker of poor prognosis

(c) retroperitoneal haemorrhage reduces the haematocrit

(d) right-to-left arterial shunting of blood in the lungs contributes to hypoxia

(e) there is distension of the transverse colon and a collapsed descending colon

4 (a) T
(b) T
(c) F
(d) T
(e) F

Internal herniation is associated with a later diagnosis and therefore a higher risk of perforation into the peritoneal cavity. These factors lead to a higher morbidity and mortality. Following prolonged vomiting the vomitus may contain faecalent fluid which consists of small bowel content and not faeces. The presence of right iliac fossa rebound tenderness and guarding is indicative of imminent or actual caecal perforation.

5 (a) T
(b) F
(c) F
(d) T
(e) T

Fat necroses are pale opaque areas found near the pancreas, greater omentum and mesentary. Lipase released causes saponification of glycerol. The fatty acids combine with calcium to form soaps. Hypocalcaemia is associated with a poor prognosis. Grey-Turner's sign (bruising in the flanks) and Cullen's sign (bruising of the periumbilical area) indicate extensive retroperitoneal haemorrhage. Additional fluid losses into the extravascular, peritoneal and pleural space contribute to the hypovolaemic shock. Right-to-left shunting in combination to oedema, splinting of the diaphragm and intravascular coagulation produce hypoxia and patients require supplemental oxygen or ventilation. A distended transverse colon and collapsed descending colon is called the 'colon cut-off' sign.

UNIT 3 ELECTIVE ABDOMINAL CONDITIONS

1 The following statements concern the anal canal:

(a) third-degree haemorrhoids are unsuitable for injection or banding

(b) submucous abscesses of the perianus lie above the dentate line

(c) squamous cell carcinoma often develops in of a long-standing fistula-in-ano

(d) annular strictures complicate Crohn's disease of the large bowel

(e) early surgery is advised in perianal Crohn's disease

2 The following are components of gallstones:

(a) calcium hydroxypalmitate

(b) protein

(c) calcium carbonate

(d) cystine

(e) calcium bilirubinate

3 In ascites:

(a) a peritoneal-jugular shunt disseminates malignancy

(b) salt intake is limited

(c) spironolactone antagonises angiotensin

(d) a milky fluid suggests chylous ascites

(e) the treatment is palliative

1 (a) T
(b) T
(c) F
(d) T
(e) F

Third-degree haemorrhoids, fibrosed haemorrhoids and failure of non-operative treatments for second-degree haemorrhoids are indications for operative management. Submucous abscesses represent approximately 5% of anorectal abscesses and by classification occur only above the dentate line. Though squamous cell carcinoma may occur in chronic fistula-in-ano this is a rare complication. Ulcerative proctitis and Crohn's disease is associated with annular strictures of the anorectum.

2 (a) F
(b) T
(c) T
(d) F
(e) T

Gallstones are classified by their composition. 90% are mixed with cholesterol as the major component. 5% are cholesterol and 5% consist solely of calcium bilirubinate. Other components include calcium carbonate, calcium phosphate, calcium palmitate and proteins.

3 (a) T
(b) T
(c) F
(d) T
(e) F

Ascites is an excess of serous fluid in the peritoneal cavity. Peritoneovenous shunts may facilitate the seeding of malignant cells at distant sites. Non-operative treatment includes dietary sodium restriction and may include diuretics. Treatment of the primary condition may reduce the portal venous pressure.

4 In portal hypertension:

(a) anastomsoses between the left gastric vein and anterior abdominal veins produce caput medusae

(b) the patient is in deep coma in CHILD's classification C

(c) magnesium sulphate reduces encephalopathy

(d) the prothrombin time is shortened

(e) barium swallow is better at revealing oesophageal varices than endoscopy

5 The following statements concern enlargements of the liver:

(a) Reidel's lobe causes only a localised swelling

(b) Budd-Chiari syndrome produces an irregular enlargement without jaundice

(c) steroids lower serum bilirubin in viral hepatitis

(d) Entamoeba histolytica pass via the portal vein to the right lobe of the liver

(e) in micronodular cirrhosis the nodules are less than 3 mm in diameter

4 (a) F
(b) T
(c) T
(d) F
(e) F

Anastomosis of the paraumbilical veins and superficial veins of the anterior abdominal wall produce caput medusae. CHILD's classification of portal hypertension is determined by the concentration of serum bilirubin, serum albumin, degree of ascites, presence of encephalopathy and prothrombin time. The presence of varices can also be demonstrated by a coeliac axis angiogram.

5 (a) T
(b) T
(c) T
(d) T
(e) T

Hepatomegaly may be generalised, localised or irregularly enlarged. The causes are numerous. In the Western world, cirrhosis, viral hepatitis and tumours are the commonest. Budd Chiari syndrome is a group of conditions with obstruction to the hepatic veins and produces a regular enlargement of the liver without jaundice. Steroids are given in patients with viral hepatitis with prolonged cholestasis to lower the serum bilirubin. Entamoeba histolytica pass from foci in the colon via the mesenteric veins and portal vein to the right lobe of the liver. Micronodular cirrhosis is characterised by nodules less than 3 mm and thick bands of fibrous tissue. It is often associated with alcohol abuse.

SYSTEM MODULE E

Urinary system and renal transplantation

UNIT 1 URINARY TRACT 1

1 Concerning urinary tract infection:

(a) incidence is lower in men due to less bacterial colonisation of the bladder

(b) repeated cystitis requires X-ray investigation only in men

(c) the leucocyte esterase test is used to detect pus cells in urine

(d) pregnant women are screened for bacteriuria and are treated if present

(e) prophylactic antibiotics are contraindicated in children

2 Haematuria:

(a) painless macroscopic haematuria is renal malignancy until proven otherwise

(b) the presence of casts containing red blood cells suggest glomerulonephritis

(c) intravenous urography is always required

(d) ultrasound is a sufficient investigation in patients under 45 years

(e) digital rectal examination is mandatory

1 (a) T
(b) F
(c) T
(d) T
(e) F

Bacterial adherence to the urothelial surface is the first step in the progress of a urinary tract infection. Colonisation and therefore infection rates are higher in women due to the shorter length of the urethra. An X-ray and ultrasound of the kidneys, ureters and bladder is indicated in cases of repeated cystitis in a woman or a single urinary tract in a male to exclude urinary stones and upper tract abnormalities. Urinary dipstick analysis is used to detect pus cells (leucocyte esterase test) and bacteria converting nitrate to nitrite (nitrate reductase test). Urinary tract infection is common in pregnancy and pyelonephritis, prior to the advent of antibiotics, was responsible for premature delivery and perinatal mortality. Pregnant women are now screened for bacteriuria at the first ante-natal visit and antibiotic prophylaxis commenced if positive. Prophylactic antibiotics are also indicated in children with more than three urinary tract infections in 6 months.

2 (a) F
(b) T
(c) F
(d) T
(e) T

Painless haematuria is the commonest presenting feature of bladder cancer which is significantly commoner than renal malignancy. Microscopy of the urine is required in haematuria as it may identify neoplastic cells casts and casts containing red blood cells that suggest glomerulonephritis. Although the gold standard in the investigation of macroscopic haematuria is an intravenous urogram this has been replaced in many centres with a plain KUB film and a renal ultrasound. Indeed many feel that ultrasonography alone is sufficient in patients under the age of 45 years with haematuria.

3 Urological trauma:

(a) 20% of abdominal trauma have associated renal trauma

(b) on table one shot IVU is indicated at laparotomy to ensure both kidneys are working

(c) renal angiography is preferred to computer tomography

(d) less than 10% of renal trauma patients require surgery

(e) the presence of blood at the urethral meatus is an indication for urethrography

4 Urinary stone disease:

(a) the absence of blood in the urine suggests an alternative diagnosis

(b) intravenous urography or USS is mandatory in all patients suspected of having stones

(c) two thirds of men will have recurrence of symptoms

(d) familiarity is an indication for metabolic screening at the first episode

(e) forced diuresis aids passage of mobile stones

5 Differential diagnosis of renal colic include:

(a) ruptured aortic aneurysm

(b) salpingitis

(c) duodenitis

(d) pyelonephritis

(e) diverticulitis

3 (a) F
(b) T
(c) F
(d) T
(e) T

10% of patients with penetrating or blunt abdominal trauma have associated renal injuries and 10% of these will require surgery. When suspected, the possibility of renal injury must be excluded if necessary with the use of one shot intravenous urography if the patient is already undergoing a laparotomy. However patients with macroscopic haematuria and shock would benefit from contrast enhanced computer tomography that is better than urography or angiography in cases of trauma. Blood at the urethral meatus requires the exclusion of urethral injury achieved by an ascending urethrogram.

4 (a) T
(b) T
(c) T
(d) T
(e) F

Urinary stones may mimic many other conditions, appendicitis, diverticulitis, salpingitis etc. The presence of symptoms in the absence of haematuria on urinary dipstick usually suggests another diagnosis but this is not absolute. The recurrence rate of urinary stone disease after one episode is between 35% and 75% at 10 years. The chances of finding a metabolic abnormality in a patient with urinary stones is small and screening is expensive. It is therefore recommended that metabolic screening be reserved for those with either a family history of stone disease or those with recurrent stones.

5 (a) T
(b) T
(c) F
(d) T
(e) T

A thorough differential diagnosis of abdominal colic-like symptoms should be borne in mind. Ruptured aortic aneurysm can mimic a renal colic surprisingly well – beware of the elderly smoker with flank pain. Pain on the right can mimic appendicitis and on the left diverticulitis.

UNIT 2 URINARY TRACT 2

1 Complications of transurethral resection of the prostate:

(a) transurethral syndrome affects less than 2% of cases

(b) incontinence occurs in 5%

(c) impotence is reported in up to 40%

(d) retrograde ejaculation occurs in more than half of all patients

(e) up to 2% mortality at 90 days

2 Prostatic carcinoma:

(a) presents with haematuria

(b) is suggested by a pronounced midline sulcus on digital rectal examination

(c) is associated with a prostatic specific antigen increase greater than 0.75 ng/ml a year

(d) has an incidence that is increasing by 3% a year

(e) localised disease in men with more than 5 years life expectancy is treated surgically

1 (a) T
(b) F
(c) T
(d) T
(e) F

The incidence of TUR syndrome in the UK is < 2% and is maintained so by the careful selection of patients and avoiding prolonged operations. The incidence of incontinence should be no greater than 1%. Impotence is indeed reported to be as high as 40% though psychological factors may contribute and the erectile dysfunction may predate the operation. The mortality at 90 days after transurethral resection of the prostate is as high as 1%. The commonest cause of death is cardiac, possibly affected by the strain of increased blood volume during and immediately following surgery.

2 (a) T
(b) F
(c) T
(d) T
(e) F

Prostatic carcinoma may present in a fashion very similar to benign prostatic hyperplasia – hesitancy, reduced stream, dribbling, nocturia and urgency. Less frequently it can present with haematuria, most commonly with the blood appearing at the beginning of micturition. Digital rectal examination is essential and may reveal an early lesion such as a nodule or later a hard craggy prostate. The median sulcus may be lost. Absolute levels of PSA can be misleading. A trend with increases of greater than 0.75 ng/ml a year suggests that the prostatic disease is not benign. Prostatic carcinoma is increasing in incidence at a rate of 3% per year, probably due the increasing life expectancy. The only hope of absolute cure of prostatic cancer is early diagnosis. Localised disease can be treated successfully by open prostatectomy in selected cases.

3 Testicular torsion:

(a) can occur at any age

(b) is commonest in infants

(c) should be diagnosed with duplex doppler to assess blood flow

(d) is the cause of 25% of acute scrotal swellings

(e) has amongst its differential diagnoses testicular tumours

4 Treatment of benign prostatic hypertrophy:

(a) laser prostatectomy is associated with retrograde ejaculation

(b) finasteride may be used successfully by dilating the bladder neck

(c) open prostatectomy is recommended for prostates greater than 100 cm^3

(d) all patients with symptoms should be treated to exclude malignancy

(e) laser prostatectomy does not allow histological evaluation of the resected specimen

5 The following statements regarding urinary retention are true:

(a) chronic retention presents with nocturnal enuresis

(b) chronic urinary retention is caused by urinary tract infection

(c) acute retention is rare in women

(d) acute retention is caused by post-operative immobility

(e) urethral catheterisation is preferred to suprapubic in chronic retention

3 (a) T
(b) F
(c) F
(d) T
(e) T

Testicular torsion can occur at any age but is commonest during adolescence. It may occasionally occur in neonates. The diagnosis of testicular torsion is clinical, investigations should not delay the exploration of the scrotum. Evidence suggests that a quarter of boys presenting with acute scrotal swelling have torsion at operation.

4 (a) F
(b) F
(c) T
(d) F
(e) T

Conventional diathermy transurethral resection of the prostate remains the gold standard for the treatment of BPH. The main advantage of laser prostatectomy is the absence of complications such as retrograde ejaculation. Its main disadvantage is that it does not allow the examination of histological specimens. Prostatectomies that require an operating time greater than 1 hour should be performed open to decrease the incidence of TUR syndrome (at present < 2%) that follows the absorption of large quantities of the irrigation fluid.

5 (a) T
(b) F
(c) T
(d) T
(e) F

Chronic urinary retention develops insidiously and is characterised by a lack of pain. Nocturnal enuresis may be a presenting feature due to overflow incontinence. Acute urinary retention is rare in women and can be caused by post-operative pain and immobility in both men and women. In chronic retention a suprapubic catheter is preferred as ascending infection is less common, bladder neck damage does not occur and 'trials without catheter' can be performed by simply clamping the catheter.

UNIT 3 RENAL FAILURE AND TRANSPLANTATION

1 Indications for renal dialysis include:

(a) hyperkalaemia ≥ 5 mmol/l

(b) pulmonary oedema

(c) metabolic acidosis

(d) Haemoglobin < 8g/dl

(e) uraemia > 50 mmol/l

2 Concerning renal dialysis:

(a) the equivalent of only 35% of renal function is provided

(b) the governing principles are of diffusion and ultrafiltration

(c) the Schribner shunt is the best method for long term access

(d) ambulatory peritoneal dialysis requires 4 times daily fluid changes

(e) infertility is a side effect

3 Brain stem death criteria:

(a) hypothermia must be excluded

(b) gag reflex is permitted in the absence of respiratory effort

(c) two medical practitioners including the transplant registrar or above are required

(d) persisting hypotension must be absent

(e) vestibulo-cochlear reflex must be absent

1 (a) F
(b) T
(c) T
(d) F
(e) T

The indications for renal dialysis are hyperkalaemia > 6.5 mmol/l, fluid overload, metabolic acidosis and uraemia > 50 mmol/l.

2 (a) F
(b) T
(c) F
(d) T
(e) T

Dialysis, based on diffusion and ultrafiltration is a means of replacing the excretory functions of failed kidneys. Most therapies provide 10% of normal renal function. The Comino shunt is an internal arterio-venous fistula that is used in long term dialysis patients. The Schribner shunt is external and is more frequently used as a short term measure. Continuous ambulatory peritoneal dialysis uses the peritoneum as a semipermeable membrane. The peritoneal cavity is filled with dialysis fluid and diffusion occurs between it and the blood stream. The dialysis fluid is changed 4 times a day. Dialysis is always second best to renal transplantation. The disadvantages of dialysis include anaemia, renal bone disease, cystic kidney change, failure to thrive in children and infertility in adults.

3 (a) T
(b) F
(c) F
(d) T
(e) T

Candidates for organ donation must be brain stem dead. This is certified by 2 independent practitioners that do not belong to the transplant team. The patient must be unresponsive with no respiratory effort. Possible other causes of apnoeic coma must be excluded such as drugs, shock, metabolic disturbance and primary hypothermia. The five brain stem reflexes including the vestibulo-cochlear reflex must be absent.

4 Renal transplantation:

(a) the donated kidney must come from a non diabetic patient

(b) central nervous system malignancies are not a contraindication to donation

(c) neurogenic bladder is a contraindication to transplantation

(d) the ureter is best placed in the bladder with a 'drop in technique'

(e) 5 year graft survival is 80%

5 Rejection:

(a) urinalysis shows proteinuria

(b) plasma IL-2 levels are raised

(c) ultrasound of the kidney shows oedema

(d) acute cellular rejection is treated with anti-thymocyte globulin before steroids

(e) cyclosporine prevents rejection by inhibiting IL-2 release

4 (a) F
(b) T
(c) T
(d) F
(e) F

The priority is that the donor kidney is normally functioning. Kidneys from diabetic patients may be used in the absence of proteinuria and with normal renal function. The donor must be absent of malignancy to avoid metastatic spread via the donated organ. The exception to this rule are central nervous system malignancies that do not metastasise. The presence of a neurogenic bladder requires the fashioning of an ileal conduit in the recipient prior to being put on the waiting list for renal transplant. However there is evidence that this may be replaced by intermittent self catheterisation. The Leadbetter-Politano technique is the method of choice for placement of the ureter into the bladder. The one year survival rate for cadaveric kidney transplantation is 70–90%.

5 (a) T
(b) T
(c) T
(d) F
(e) T

The clinical findings in rejection are tenderness over the graft, pyrexia, reduced urine output and signs of fluid retention. Investigation of the urine will reveal proteinuria. Blood tests will reveal a raised urea, white cell count and IL-2 level. An ultrasound of the kidney will reveal oedema and possibly evidence of obstruction of the system. The first line treatment of acute cellular rejection is pulsed methylprednisolone. Steroid resistant cellular rejection may be treated with anti-thymocyte globulin. Immunosuppression is achieved by combinations of steroids, Azathioprine, Cyclosporine A and antibodies. Prednisolone decreases IL-1 production, azathioprine interferes with messenger RNA and DNA production and cyclosporine inhibits IL-2 release and spares suppressor cells.

TIPS FOR THE VIVA VOCE EXAMINATION

This is a test of the candidate's ability to apply their knowledge while under the pressure of the exam. It is a test of attitude and presentation as much as knowledge.

Dress and attitude

Be clean, smart and conservative. The smell of the most fashionable after shave or cigarettes carries no weight in the Royal College of Surgeons.

Be confident but humble. You may know more about the fine details of the action of pH dependent anti-inflammatory drugs in ulcerative colitis than your orthopaedic examiner but do not be smug. The examiner is always right; if he is not his colleague is there to correct him or her.

Speak slowly in clear English; avoid colloquialisms, hospital slang or abbreviations.

Under direct questioning it is vital to reply with structured answers to avoid going off the point. There are a limited number of types of questions available to the examiner. Preparing a structured approach to each of these types of question will improve the clarity of your answers. The key words are *manage, assess, diagnose, investigate, causes of,* or involve a *procedure.* Practice with the different permutations reveals that the schemes repeat themselves. The following are examples of question structure and a technique for answering.

How do you 'manage' a condition

Management includes all aspects of the medical care of a particular condition from presentation to discharge. All other clinical questions – assessment, diagnosis etc are a greater or lesser fragment of this. In an out-patient setting management always begins with a history. In the answer to management of an acute presentation, resuscitation takes priority and the history is described as either contemporaneous or subsequent to management of the life threatening conditions.

Resuscitation	Airways (with cervical spine control)
	Breathing
	Circulation
	Disability (neurosurgical emergencies and trauma)
	Exposure (trauma)

The degree of emphasis and detail required should be tailored to the condition. For example, an acute abdomen or a multiply injured patient will require a more extensive account of resuscitative method.

History and examination

There are a number of possible approaches. The salient symptoms and signs may be initially listed with a short statement on each of and their relevance . Alternatively, the 'clinical features' – the key points in both the history and examination – are described.

In the case of 'how would you manage a 50 year old alcoholic with cirrhosis' one would start the answer presenting a basic outline of your approach: 'I would take a full history and examine the patient' – a simple answer that can be applied to every question of this type. However, as stated above, had the question been on the management of an alcoholic with an upper gastrointestinal bleed the answer would begin with resuscitation.

The next step is to describe the features in the history and examination that are relevant. For example 'in the history I would specifically enquire about a history of vomiting blood, jaundice, dark urine and a history of abdominal distention (ascites) as well as taking a dietary history' etc. Remember that if the examiner wishes to know a detail he or she will ask; this is preferable to listing endless details that may leave little time for further discussion.

In the examination begin with inspection as in practice. Hence, 'on general examination I would seek the systemic features of liver disease' (palmar erythema, flap, gynaecomastia, spider naevi, ascites etc). Further possible signs to find on examination are then mentioned such as hard liver, ascites etc.

Reassurance and analgesia

In the discussion of an out patient case one would now move onto the investigations; in an acute presentation, reassurance and analgesia take priority and demonstrate that a patient is being discussed rather than a disease. The use of strong opiate analgesia is still contentious; however, in general, once a working diagnosis has been established it is now considered reasonable and humanitarian to administer strong analgesics. Traditionalists may contest this in an exam scenario but omission is now probably more deleterious than inclusion.

Investigations

A recurring theme is that of structure and classification that will demonstrate the clarity of thought needed in surgical practice. Investigations may be basic or special and the division into departments may help avoid forgetting essential investigations.

Remember that investigations are for diagnosis, severity (or staging) and to asses fitness for surgery. To actually state this may act as an aide memoir. When possible offer a sentence of explanation for each investigation indicating a possible finding or the logic for the test, eg in a patient awaiting a nephrectomy for malignancy you may request a chest radiograph 'to help exclude metastases and assess fitness for surgery'. Equally in preparing a patient for a hip replacement a full blood count may reveal a leucocytosis suggestive of occult infection which could contraindicate surgery or chronic blood loss secondary to a non-steroidal induced peptic bleed.

Simple

Urinalysis	eg dip stick bilirubin
Haematology	eg full blood count
Biochemistry	eg urea and electrolytes
Radiological	eg plain films

Special

It helps to start with the least invasive and most inexpensive investigations. A classification into departments is good for clarity. Hence talk of a differential blood count before ultrasonography and before mentioning magnetic resonance imaging. When possible offer an explanation or the reasoning behind the choice of investigations unless this is obvious.

Following the resuscitation, history, examination and investigations there is sufficient information to:

1. Establish the diagnosis
2. Determine severity of disease (stage in malignancy)
3. Assess fitness for surgery
4. Plan treatment

Treatment

Treatment of surgical disorders can be either non-operative or operative. The follow-up required should always be mentioned.

In the treatment one should consider both the local disease, the distant spread (where appropriate) and the systemic effects.

Surgical disorders require an holistic approach with the use of a multidisciplinary team. Consideration of the psychological and social needs of the patient as well as the physical will demonstrate a complete understanding of the pathology and its effects.

Non-operative treatment includes simple reassurance with follow-up, physiotherapy, pharmacological therapy including cytotoxic chemotherapy, radiotherapy, immunotherapy and hormonal manipulation. The latter of these may be used in conjunction with surgery where they are termed adjuvant or neo-adjuvant depending on whether they follow or precede surgery.

Surgery may be curative, palliative or reconstructive

Curative surgery in malignancy implies the removal of all macroscopic disease in the absence of distant spread. It also implies the complete removal of secondary deposits, eg a hepatic lobectomy for colonic carcinoma metastases.

Palliative surgery is applied to those cases where cure is not an option. The indications include pain, obstruction and blood loss.

Reconstructive surgery aims to restore both form and function whether deficient due to the primary disease or to the subsequent therapy.

Summary

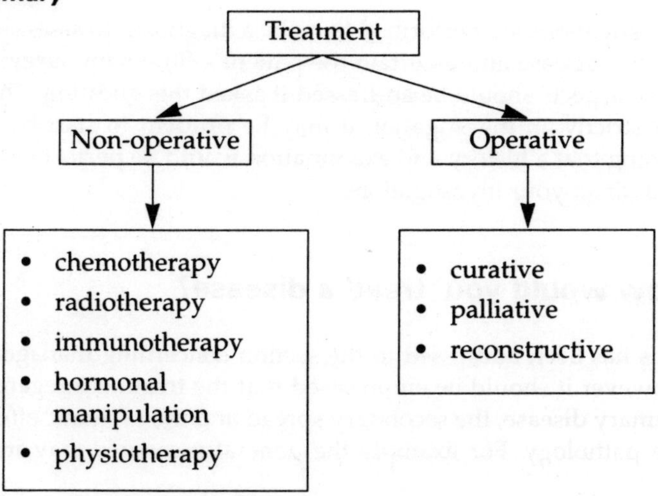

Discharge and follow-up of the patient includes the mechanisms for return to the community (primary care, physiotherapy, occupational therapy and social services). Consideration should be given to the intervals for review and the necessary basic and special investigations that should be performed for surveillance.

How do you 'assess' a condition?

Assessment involves the diagnosis (see below) of a disease and its severity. In malignant disease the severity of disease corresponds to the stage. In non malignant disease various parameters are used eg Ranson criteria in acute pancreatitis, or Child's classification of liver impairment.

How do you 'diagnose' a condition?

Diagnosis requires taking a history and examination followed by basic and special investigations. This does not include the assessment of severity and need not be mentioned unless requested by the examiner.

How do you 'investigate' a condition?

Investigations are performed to make a diagnosis, to assess severity of a disease and ascertain the patient's fitness for surgery. All these aspects should be addressed if asked this question. Though not strictly an investigation it may be prudent to start by mentioning that a history and examination would be performed. This will direct your investigations.

How would you 'treat' a disease?

This has been addressed in the section concerning management. However it should be emphasised that the treatment regards the primary disease, the secondary spread and the systemic effects of the pathology. For example the general measures may include nutritional support of cachectic patients and blood transfusion in anaemia secondary to chronic disease.

The standard scheme of discussing the non-operative and the operative treatments with their respective subdivisions is always applied.

Tell me about a procedure or a technique

These questions can lead to confused answers if a basic framework is not used. The following is a structure for approaching questions about colonoscopy, chest drainage, audit and screening.

Definition

A succinct explanation of what the technique entails.

Indications

For procedures these may be elective/emergency and/or investigative/therapeutic.

Method

A chronological commentary on the consent and preparation of the patient, the type of anaesthesia, followed by a stepwise account of the procedure. Do not become stuck on minor details.

Advantages and disadvantages

Discuss briefly the pros and cons of the procedure or technique.

Complications

These are divided into local and general. Both of these are then considered as immediate, early or late.

General

These include the complications of anaesthesia, be it local, regional or general.

Immediate	at or soon after the procedure
Early	during the post-operative stay on the ward or intensive care unit
Late	after discharge from the hospital

Specific

Immediate

Early

Late

Operative viva

When describing an operation consider:

- resuscitation (in acute conditions including appendicectomy)
- pre-operative preparation (including DVT and antibiotic prophylaxis)
- consent
- position of the patient on the operating table
- personal scrubbing, gowning and gloving
- skin preparation and draping

Be prepared to go into detail on any of these preliminaries. For example what do you use to scrub and for how long? What do you prepare the skin with and why? Do you adopt DVT prophylaxis for perianal abscesses? What are your gloves and gown made of? And so on.

Now you may begin with your skin incision. Give the salient points of the operation and go into detail only when asked. If not interrupted, continue to the end of the operation. The operation ends when the patient is fully awake.